HONEY, WE F*CKED UP THE KIDS!

A step-by-step process on how to be a less sh!tty parent

MATTHEW MAYNARD, LMFT

Copyright © 2023 Matthew Maynard, LMFT

All rights reserved. Without limiting the rights under copyright reserved above, no part of this publication may be reproduced, stored in, or introduced into a retrieval system, or transmitted, in any form, or by any means without the prior written permission of the author.

ISBN 979-8-9889719-0-0 (paperback)
ISBN 979-8-9889719-1-7 (ebook)

I dedicate this book…

To my father who has taught me how to persevere through the worst parts of life. To my mother who taught me to love deeply. To my incredible wife who unwaveringly supports me in my insanity. To my incredible children Mason and Mila who teach me how to be a less shitty parent.

This is for you.

Contents

About the Author.. vii

Introduction.. ix

Chapter 1. Where's the village?........................ 1
Chapter 2. You Get to Kinda Blame Your Family of Origin!.... 16
Chapter 3. Your Own Sh*t Now........................... 34
Chapter 4. The Insane Power of Rapport Building......... 43
Chapter 5. Compliance/Problems Vs Principles/Accountability........ 58
Chapter 6. Highly Effective Strategies To Be Less Shitty..... 74
Chapter 7. Unhealthy Boundaries to Stop Doing........... 95
Chapter 8. Taking Responsibility and Setting a New Normal for Hierarchy...... 107
Chapter 9. Strategic Leverage vs Traditional Consequences/Punishment........ 116
Chapter 10. Where Do Less Shitty Parents Go From Here?... 133

References... 141

About the Author

Matt Maynard is a Licensed Marriage and Family therapist currently in private practice in both Fairfield County, CT and Bergen County, NJ. He has been working with burnt out parents to create sustainable and healthy approaches to raising kids that will have pride, character, and self sufficiency to live their dreams. He was tired of all the academic and unsustainable parenting approaches that were well intentioned, but short sighted on behavior change only. Matt set out to develop his own program called Emotionally Strategic Parenting, which is entirely focused on creating healthy family hierarchy's, personal accountability, and strategic consequences for kids to have more empowerment and self-esteem. He currently coaches parents across America who are looking to parent smarter, not harder. If you want to learn more about him, go to www.bio.site/mattmaynard

Introduction

I'm glad you're here. There are two things I want you to know. One, the perfect parent does not exist. And two, you are not alone. Whatever you have seen on social media, the news, and through the hundreds of parenting books that you may have read, gives you the impression that parenting perfection is possible. I am here to blow that myth completely out of the water. Take comfort in the notion that you are not alone. All the struggles, and the immense responsibility that comes along with raising another human life is insanely stressful. Honestly, you probably feel like every parent I have worked with…shitty.

Do you find yourself feverishly consuming every parenting article you can find on the internet, or is your bookshelf filled to the top with parenting books that just haven't seemed to give you the guidance you so desperately need? And now you're feeling even more confused and frustrated than when you began. It makes sense, because the strategies and insight you have been getting only focus on the behavior, or even worse, it makes you feel guilty for not loving your kids enough.

Here is something else I want you to know: it is possible to have both a positive relationship with your child while also being able to guide their behavior through the powerful use of consequences, without power struggles. That's right…no more power struggles. No more screaming, yelling, threatening, or lecturing. I am going to give you a system on how to do just that!

Hang on to your hat; in the world of parenting, reward systems do not work for instilling character. They only get in the way. Reward systems stop superficial behavior changes, meaning they will stop the behavior (possibly), but only on the surface. They don't address the internal root of behavior. The result when using a reward system is that you become overwhelmed, and your kid becomes confused and disheartened.

Ultimately, your child will go out into a world looking for external validation, rather than internal motivation. Meaning they will seek out validation from their environments, instead of having the tools they need within themselves.

Each of these steps cannot be entirely accomplished by the end of this book, unless you are okay with settling, right now, for being less shitty. Frankly this is probably the best a parent will feel; that they are capable in today's insanely busy, stressful, and influential world.

That's right. You have to be okay with being less shitty in your parenting so you can drop the guilt. Stop the shame of not being the picture-perfect social media influencer mom who tells you that your kids just need you to spend more time with them, love them more, and focus on more special bonding. Nothing against this advice as I honestly want this for you, but too much of anything good can turn toxic. I can help you turn the tide if you've bought into this mom guilt.

I will disprove the nonsense myths that I know you have come to love from those motivational social media influencers (I am being sarcastic; I really mean hate), the endless rewards and sticker charts, endless amounts of praising and aggrandizing. I'll address the never-ending sadness and guilt that comes with feeling as though you need to yell or be mean to get your kids to listen. I will explain why all of these completely silly beliefs come from an outdated, albeit well-intentioned behavioral focus of children, none of which I am willing to be a part of professionally. And I know for a fact, once you're done with this book you will not follow it as well.

First, let's talk about what shitty parenting really means. Because of course, we need to understand it before we can even begin to understand what LESS shitty parenting is all about. *Shitty parenting is...*

- believing that getting your kids to listen and obey your commands will help them be happier and less stressed. That is until you work yourself further into a job to micromanage your kids...a job that less shitty parents work themselves out of.
- focusing on your child's outcomes and as a result minimizing how they got there. *How you make a million dollars matters more than the million dollars you make!*
- believing that the kids' behavior and successes are a direct reflection of who you are and what you have done as a parent. This is well intentioned, but leads to broken boundaries.
- believing that fear, intimidation, and compliance are a means to create a well-adjusted and respectful child to authority. Sometimes parents even believe that hitting

them is what is required because that's what they got when they were a kid.
- believing that rewards and positive emotions are the pathway to the child developing a sense of self-esteem and feeling pride in their process. (Completely unsustainable and exhausting for the parents).
- believing that you need to have their back and constantly accommodate their feelings when others are hurtful, mean, or unfair.
- believing that any consequence or negative outcome is punitive and hurtful to the child's ability to develop a sense of self or worse, destroying the parent-child bond.
- focusing only on the problems the child faces and viewing these problems as threats.

Now, let's look at less shitty parenting...

- believing that your kids are capable of thinking and learning from reflection after they have had independence, to a certain degree, and learning over time from their mistakes. Working themselves out of the job of manager.
- focusing on your child's process of *how* they get their outcomes rather than only on the outcomes themselves. *How* you make a million dollars matters more than the million dollars you make!

- believing that your kids' behaviors and successes are a direct reflection of *who they are* becoming and learning to build into their character. <u>Healthy boundaries</u>!
- believing that encouragement, emotional validation, and accountability are a means to create a well-adjusted and respectful child, that both gains and gives respect to authority.
- believing that rewards and positive emotions are good with delayed gratification for big accomplishments. And that achievements are the pathway to the child developing a sense of self-esteem and feeling pride in their process. (Sustainable and easier for parents to implement).
- believing that you can emotionally validate and understand your child's emotional pain, while not accommodating or enabling them to feel better when others are hurtful, mean, or unfair.
- believing that consequences and negative outcomes are a temporary discomfort that can be utilized to reflect and create healthy anxiety within a child to not repeat again and have future success for pride.
- focus on instilling principles during problems so that the child is learning what is appropriate to do in the future.

These are just a *few* of the ideas I am going to dispel throughout this book. I will give you the EXACT, step-by-step insight on how to approach my parenting system to achieve what *every* parent ultimately wants for their children, to help them with character development; to live with principles; and to have self-esteem and pride in their process. Character and integrity are at the heart of what successful, less shitty parents focus on.

Right now, you may have to come to terms with the fact that you are going to be an outcast from all the other moms and dads out there. The strategies and approaches that I am going to recommend throughout this book are going to trigger and piss off *a lot* of people, including at times you and even your own parents! I hope, though, that you will stick with me and start to rebel against these negative feelings. I hope you choose to instead grow to become a less shitty parent that is focused more on developing character instead of falling for short term behavioral change.

Chapter 1

WHERE'S THE VILLAGE?

Remember how I just said that you are going to have to get more comfortable being an outcast, *whelp, buckle up buckaroos* because it's going to be lonely for a little while. There is a saying that *it takes a village to raise a child*. This is true, except the reality is the village has gone dark. Very dark. The 'village', meaning other parents, schools, and authority figures (to name a few) have been overwhelmed. Resources have greatly diminished due to the amount of stress parents have been under. Also take into consideration the fact that these systems have been deeply underappreciated, undervalued, and disrespected.

In turn this has led to a significant sense of anxiety and insecurity for these systems to become involved, as they themselves get sucked into the conflicts and problems (to the point that they become the scapegoat). I have seen it in my own practice and even know clinicians and other counselors who refuse to stand up and give the difficult feedback that parents <u>need</u> to start to hear. I hope that if you have stuck with me to this point, you are open minded enough to hear me out. If you want the village's assistance with your kid, start to give them the liberty to do so. Kids are raised now in environments where they are led to believe that they have some incredible amount of power and sway within these adult systems, when they shouldn't. We have let the *inmates run the asylum.*

My recommendation is to show your village that they have your support and explicitly tell them that you want them to be able to use their authority to influence and shape your child's behavior. Tell them that you want them to be able to set limits and consequences in school in order for your child to become exposed to difficult situations and stress from others outside their home. I promise some of your village will go into overdrive for you, because often they air more on the side of caution than they actually feel like they can do their jobs.

Partial Parenting Myths

If you have read any parenting book or listened to some parenting podcasts you are going to run into two main ideas. The first is that the emotional attachment that you have with your kids is not closely bonded enough; that more needs to be done (by you) to allow your child to feel more emotionally comforted by you. The second is that you need to calmly explain problematic behaviors and set consequences in order to get your child incentivized/rewarded, thus encouraging a behavior change.

These two things are not entirely untrue…sometimes parents do need to establish a closer emotional relationship and they need to positively reward behavior. When the child is very young, love and connection are important. Incentives and rewards do help. The unfortunate reality is you, like all the parents I have worked with, have done these steps. Followed this advice. Not just a little, but a ton! You are still here reading this book and scratching your head as to why your kids are still acting out. These strategies are unsustainable and unrealistic. At some point the kids need to detach and they need to recognize that the world is not meant to incentivize them, because, as we know, it rarely does that! This is another reason why most parents feel that they are doing a shitty job. I promise that if you are the kind of person that would pick this book up, buy it, and get to this point, you are more than likely too good of a parent. Here is what I mean.

There is such a thing as being too good of a parent…and the good news is if you're reading this book, that's been your main problem.

The reality is that kids are too emotionally entangled or dependent on their parents to the point where you don't know who is emotionally or physically responsible for who anymore. The boundary is completely broken. The other reality is the parents are so focused on changing behavior, that the kids look to please their parents just enough to get what they want. Or they may engage in terrorist-like behaviors to beat down already burnt-out parents. The kids may even get the parents to fight one another about their approach or what they did wrong. Does this feel like you right now? Does this nightmare sound familiar? If so, great! I know this book can help you.

How did we get here as a society?

Parents have become insecure and anxious about their abilities. They are constantly fearful of judgment and criticism because of the aforementioned lack of a village. Instead, now the village has become judgmental and critical to the point where we are doubting or creating self-limiting beliefs. This has resulted in us being more personally and emotionally invested in our kids than ever before.

I have real case examples where parents are hovering over the *Find my iPhone* app trying to navigate their kids going to a friend's house. Some are even still brushing their kids teeth for them…at age 10. They are doing assignments and writing papers for them…as juniors in prestigious, high end boarding schools. They are even calling or emailing college professors…. that's right, college professors. This is painful to watch and is creating a future and present generation of emotionally immature adults. They are entering the world with limited stress tolerance and have expectations of receiving far more than they are willing to give. Young adults believe others are more responsible, both physically and emotionally, for them than they are. When I speak with most of them, their level of spite and vindictiveness when they don't get their way is mind blowing. It's even to a degree of self-sabotage, believing that they are getting back at their parents. Some of you reading this know exactly what I am talking about.

Not only that, we have kids that are now more emotionally and mentally unhealthy than at any other time in recorded human history, even though we are living in one of the most prosperous times.

1. Rates of depression in adolescents have increased by 30% over the past decade, according to a study published in the Journal of the American Medical Association (Rao et al., 2020).
2. A 2019 report by the American Psychological Association found that rates of anxiety among teenagers have been steadily increasing over the past few decades, with 70% of Gen Z teens saying that anxiety and depression are major issues among their peers (American Psychological Association, 2019).
3. The National Survey on Drug Use and Health found that the percentage of adolescents reporting a major depressive episode increased from 8.7% in 2005 to 13.3% in 2018 (Substance Abuse and Mental Health Services Administration, 2019).
4. A study published in the journal Pediatrics found that the suicide rate for children aged 10-14 has nearly tripled since 2007 (Bridge et al., 2018).
5. The number of children and teens who have been diagnosed with ADHD has been steadily increasing over the past two decades, with the Centers for Disease Control and Prevention reporting that the prevalence of ADHD among children aged 6-17 increased from 7.8% in 2003 to 10.2% in 2016 (Centers for Disease Control and Prevention, 2019).

6. Rates of anxiety, depression, and self-harm are higher among adolescents who spend more than 3 hours a day on social media, according to a study published in the journal JAMA Psychiatry (Lin et al., 2019).

Times have drastically changed and the present moment of how parents, educators, therapists, and other professionals are enabling, accommodating, and pandering to children has gone too far. We are not creating kids that are resilient and have integrity in the choices and behavior they exhibit that will create pride. It is emotionally and physically imperative for kids to grow into adults who do more than just survive, who thrive into people with strong character, values, and morals. It has been my mission to address this headfirst with all my clients and I hope that you will stay along for the ride throughout the book, because I am going to give you no bullshit strategies to be able to address this with both love and firm accountability. We are going to go beyond just superficial behavior and surface level problems and instead get to building proud people. But first, how the hell did we get here?

What led to this major shift?

To better understand we need to go to parenting back in the day...for some of you that is when parents were able to hit their kids. (Please note I am not advocating for that!) See back when most of the parents that I work with were growing up, they were raised during the 60's, 70's and 80's. Parenting then was substantially different! Kids were seen and not heard. Most of them were physically and emotionally abused through punishment and compliance based on today's standards. Name calling, guilt/shame, and intimidation were tactics that most of the clients I work with experienced the most, although some didn't experience any of these things. Some had great childhoods and very close and loving relationships with their parents, learning to please and follow directions. This however sounds great until they struggle to have their own sense of emotional integrity and live a life based on others' beliefs, expectations, and validation.

Often, if you wanted to have a relationship with a parent, you had to amalgamate around *their* hobbies in *their* areas of interest and there was a substantial amount of pleasing and compliance. Most parents that I work with are presently still trying to oscillate between these two approaches of pleasing their children while also trying to use outdated compliance-based parenting approaches.

Teachers and school administrators could physically hit you back then. They could call you out in class, send you to the office to be reprimanded. Teachers would call home and report the behaviors that they experienced with kids in class. The saying "wait until your father gets home," was common. I am not advocating for the world and parents to go back to this approach. There were a ton of unintended consequences to this approach, and I am a staunch believer of not using physical punishment or force to gain compliance from children. *Compliance is the last thing I am going to show you that you want to get from your kids*!

These experiences shaped a ton of the parenting approaches that have shifted over the past 30-50 years. When these kids grew up, they were trying to shift parenting to be more emotionally attuned to children and around attachment. This led to a whole entire subset of parenting books about the emotional well-being of children and the focus on kids feeling good about themselves. This was a positive shift from the one that many grew accustomed to and accepting of when they were kids. Books and professionals started to tout the power of love, attachment, and reward systems. Sticker charts, nesting, and putting the bond of the parent-child relationship above everything else were concepts that started to become integrated into all aspects of children's experiences. As a result, this led to a prioritization of artificially and substantially cushioning the child's experience so that they could experience success consistently, while never fearing the loss of the parental relationship. This all sounded incredible, so everyone jumped on the bandwagon!

Trophies for participating is the easy one everyone talks about now, but this is just the tip of the iceberg based on what I am seeing and experiencing as a professional. We are now passing kids through grades that they are literally failing, because we don't want to hurt their feelings. We are giving them resources and accommodations and watering down expectations, setting them up to believe that the world will work around them and their feelings.

This gigantic shift has swung too far... *kids are now seen, heard, excessively listened to, prioritized over the other parent, accommodated, incentivized, and cajoled for everyday normal stressors.* We as adults have also gotten very accustomed to things being emotionally easy and streamlined due to smartphones that we literally live and die by now. Patience and delay are a concept of the distant past. We don't even have to wait in line anymore at the coffee shop because we can order ahead. You don't need to hail a cab anymore; a nicer, cleaner, and cheaper fare pulls up directly beside you. It's both incredible and terrifying all at the same time because these little instances of waiting or being flexible to outside stressors is almost completely gone from children, and the parents I work with. *Anything that is worth doing and has value takes time, persistence, and perseverance.*

    I used this example in a session with a teenager I had the other day. I asked him, "how long does it take you to load a website you like to go on?" His response, "3 seconds." I then went on to explain to him that when I was his exact age, that same process would take 8-12 steps that were structured around a lot of different factors such as someone picking up the phone while you were online. *Remember that?* Remember what happened if someone picked up the phone after you spent 20 minutes just finally getting your computer comfortable enough to start dialing up. If that happened your computer would have a massive seizure and demand you to force shutdown by pulling the plug and starting the process over again. Because just starting up my family desktop computer, not a laptop, a desktop, took anywhere between 5-10 minutes. Factor in another 3-5 minutes for AOL (America Online) to startup and not have an error. To then patiently wait for the home screen to load and pray that you didn't accidently click on anything because the computer could only do one thing at a time.

    You see, these small challenges of perseverance, inconvenience, and despair *were* normal. NORMAL! This was something that you had to work around and work through. This wasn't artificial either. It was based on an intrinsic motivation to do something that you desired to do. Wanted to play video games with a friend? You needed a ride, or you needed to ride your bike to their house.

You had to try calling them on their house phone to see if they were even home. You had to be able to then wait and pray to God that they would call you back and you were near the phone, or someone wasn't on the phone keeping the line busy... *you see where I'm going with this?*

Then normal life required more steps. More external factors to work around and be flexible with. Patience and managing disappointment when it didn't pan out. Resilience was slowly and never-endingly built into desires and goals.

Now listen, I am not trying to say that I'm ungrateful for the advances in technology and the convenience of all of this. For instance, I'm a complete coffee addict. Seriously, the less time it takes for that to hit my bloodstream the better! What I am trying to say, though, is that now I'm realizing how little stress-tolerance I have as a grown adult man. It is something that now has to be worked on. It has to be pressing and at the top of the mind, because if not, it is so easy to get sucked right back into the hole and lose sight of the grit and resilience that is needed to live an emotionally deep and rich life; one that has quality and connection. One that has massive accomplishment and contribution to the world. One to be proud of.

The Importance of Family Hierarchy of Emotionally Focused Parenting Approaches

The family hierarchy as a functional structural system is <u>*not*</u> something that is deeply discussed in other parenting programs, books, or podcasts. I can imagine that it is usually boring, mega-complex, and really difficult to talk about through a book instead of a conversation. Not only that, these individuals continue to believe that focusing on the child's emotional experience over everything else is of utmost importance. Let's talk about the distinct differences though the importance of a hierarchy over being emotionally focused on attachment.

One reason why having a parental hierarchy is important is that it helps children develop a sense of order and structure. When parents establish clear rules and expectations, children learn to respect authority and understand that their actions have consequences. That means when they make great choices, they feel empowered and get to keep all the credit! In emotionally focused parenting, the emphasis is often on the child's emotions, which can lead to a lack of discipline and structure in the home and beyond. Not only that, it leads them to falsely believe that others in the world will also do the same. We are seeing this presently play out in society in regard to freedom of speech. Something that's incredibly important.

Another reason why a parental hierarchy is beneficial is that it teaches children important life skills, such as decision-making and problem-solving. When parents take on the role of establishing limits and consequences, they can guide their children in making responsible choices and learning from their mistakes. In contrast, emotionally focused parenting may prioritize the child's feelings over their ability to make good decisions. Once again, believing that ultimately, they may not be responsible for the consequences of their actions, setting them up for a world outside that does not exist.

Having a parental hierarchy also promotes a sense of security and stability for children. When parents establish themselves as the primary authority figures, children feel safe and secure knowing that their parents are in control and can protect them. In emotionally focused parenting, the focus on the child's emotions can sometimes lead to a lack of structure and consistency, which can create anxiety and uncertainty for children. Also, it reaffirms the belief that others will always protect and insulate them from experiences, people, and conflicts that they may be immature to manage.

Overall, this focus on parental hierarchy being important has far more benefits to assist kids in transitioning from the family dynamic into the macro dynamic of the real world. The transition is not going to further create anxiety, fear, depression, or a sense of trust in others, setting them up to more than likely be taken advantage of. Not only this, but it also has a significant reduction in kids believing that they are entitled to certain privileges and luxuries, resulting in them developing a stronger work ethic and belief in themselves that they can make their life better.

A lot of attachment-based parenting books have highlighted benefits from some of these scenarios. I can tell you from professional experience that these benefits are short-term and misguided in building up children to be confident, well adjusted, young adults. The path to hell is paved with good intentions. Children crying, being upset, disappointed, and disheartened is appropriate and necessary for them to learn to cope with their emotions. *I call this process normalizing the negatives.* Shitty parents have the false belief that if any of these emotions are present in their children that they are "failing" or "not loving" them. Less shitty parents recognize that these experiences are necessary for them to learn how to adapt, take responsibility, and learn to grow so that they will not fall back into the same patterns in the future. They recognize these experiences as something that can help the child to create healthy anxiety and emotional anchors that can serve them in the future. These experiences are the building blocks for how character and pride is built.

The less shitty parenting way!

Alright we know how we got to become far too good of a parent, we realize that the world today is going to require a vastly different parenting approach because stress tolerance isn't built in, and the old ways and even the newest of ways are unsustainable… so, let's be less shitty!

Elements that make this approach deeply different compared to others…

1. We are going to start focusing more on principles instead of problems. This means that we are going to focus on bigger ideas and concepts than detailed behaviors. That means no more arguing around content and details. Also, kids love bigger ideas as small nuances are going to get lost on them. Less is more here. This also is more about positive learning instead of negative hostility.
2. We are going to focus on intrinsic motivation and character instead of conditional behavior change. That means we are no longer incentivizing, rewarding, and keeping track of stickers for sticker charts. Kids are going to start to make changes because of the kind of person *they want to be* rather than what they might get in the short term. We are focused on them making choices

because of *how it makes them feel about themselves*, not what is in it for themselves. Smells like narcissism.

3. We are empowering the kids to learn from their mistakes and create their own strategies to overcome challenges. This means no more lecturing which is highly ineffective and exhausting for parents. Also, this allows the kids to start to feel in control and empowered with their own decisions. They do more of the heavy lifting and reap the benefits from their eventual success. We instead ask emotionally reflective questions to promote having the child open up and process their feelings, while also balancing out how they are going to appropriately respond in the future, thus shaping happy, healthy people instead of training dogs to not pee in the house.

4. We are using consequences in a strategic and delayed fashion to reduce power struggles and create a healthy authority within the family hierarchy. Consequences and punishments are two vastly different things. Punishments are personal, whereas consequences are ramifications to a choice the child makes. This allows for a stronger boundary and healthy separation between the child and the parent(s). Kids feel more secure in systems where they make more choices and decisions some of the time, instead of trying to control or power struggle their way through.

5. We use attention and engagement more sparingly because kids need to understand that they are not always worthy of receiving this. Attention and engagement

are like money to kids. They love it, can't get enough of it, and believe that they are always owed more! We are going to start to look at using these two aspects of parenting more sparingly as they are extremely powerful, but very expensive for parents. Remember that less is more here people!

6. Finally, we are going to shift our entire focus to be about holding kids more accountable for their choices rather than being compliant of our demands. Less shitty parents are focused on getting their kids to learn to think for themselves rather than listening and following other people. This shift is massive and allows you to free up more resources for yourself, help break the never-ending pattern of "being needed" and helps establish a stronger sense of self-esteem in your kids. Their choices are their own successes or failures, listening and following directions leads to them being victims or not good enough. Not only that, aren't you tired of being blamed or hearing, "why didn't you remind me?"

With all that being said, and if you're still with me, we're ready to dive in…hang on tight, it's going to be a wild ride.

Chapter 2

YOU GET TO KINDA BLAME YOUR FAMILY OF ORIGIN!

In order to understand this chapter as a whole, I want to start by discussing unconscious patterns in relationships and how this self-awareness is powerful to create connection again. These patterns can be unintentionally damaging to relationship dynamics, as they are meant to protect us from past experiences or help motivate us to respond in certain ways that were helpful in the past. However, these patterns were based on circumstances and dynamics that are from a different period in time and rarely fit the current situation. It is essential to bring these unconscious thoughts to the forefront of the conscious mind so you can start to be less shitty.

We need to explore the ways these past experiences color your perception of your own child and lead you to respond. We are all unconsciously projecting, meaning placing (or displacing) our own unwanted feelings and desires, which blurs boundaries and responsibilities. We want to give meaning to the dynamics within our family. The goal is to gain awareness around this, and to recognize projection when/if it's happening. My gut leads me to believe it IS more likely than not. I am biased, though.

Most therapists tend to avoid this area, because they are fearful of how it will be received by parents. The fear is that you will become defensive or guarded and interpret this as all your fault. Regardless of the strategies I give you, these unconscious beliefs will deeply lead to reactivity and continue to perpetuate the conflict cycle. Please be gracious and patient with yourself in this process, as it can be emotionally painful and difficult to look at the past. Remember we are no longer focused on being perfect. No pressure! This chapter will highlight why you may struggle with implementing some strategies that I will outline. And it's important to get clarification in this area in order to utilize the strategies effectively.

We will start by taking a deeper look at your own childhood, and how that plays a role in shaping you as the shitty parent you are today. "Matt, does that mean I get to blame my parents?!?" Kinda! We will discover areas in your own childhood that were difficult or happy, therefore leading to you being hyper-focused on these areas in your child. For example, this includes being bullied, assaulted, low self-esteem, low motivation, and so on.

We'll explore the role you had in your own family of origin and whether you are still maintaining this role which can have a negative influence on your child. You'll consider the family culture in which you grew up in and how this has influenced specific beliefs and perspectives you have now. We'll take a deeper look at explaining how guilt and shame was possibly a motivator for you as a child. You will begin to identify the unhealthy relationship dynamics of this as it leads to an inability to individuate in a healthy manner. You'll begin to identify people and patterns that you see within your child or fear that your children will act like that you may have experienced in your own life, for example: brothers, sisters, uncles, mother, father, physical aggressors, limited motivated sibling, suicidal or completed suicide family member, peers who may have been drug users etc.

As you work through these realizations, you will also begin to identify unhealthy boundaries and begin to clarify emotional enmeshment that you more than likely have with your kids. Emotional enmeshment is where the emotions, responsibilities, and problem-solving boundaries are blurred, in this case, between a parent and child, and turn into one instead of two distinct people. This leads to escalating conflicts, parenting resentment, anxiety, and insecurity around self-esteem, as well as a sense of narcissism and entitlement.

By looking at your own childhood and position within your family, you can start to explore additional relationship pressures leading to either enmeshment or hostility within current parenting strategies. For example, your own parents, in-laws, brothers/sisters, spouse, and so on may be affecting how you are parenting your own children.

An aspect that you may not realize affects you as a parent is your personal relationship with your spouse, or lack thereof. We will explore the benefits of prioritizing your marriage over your children and how this affects the emotional well-being of your child. And along with that we will explore other personal areas that are currently problematic and how these may contribute to an attitude or approach toward your child. Some of these include marital discord, financial stressors, health related complications, divorce.

Finally, and this may be the most difficult piece of the puzzle for some, you'll be able to recognize the need for your own support. You'll realize the benefit of processing your own pain through individual psychotherapy, family therapy, marriage counseling or a support group (AA, Al-Anon, etc).

Family of Origin

Let's begin by talking about unconscious patterns in relationships and how this self-awareness is powerful to create connection once again. The good old Freudian stuff! I want you to think back specifically on your childhood to areas or events that were particularly painful or emotionally fulfilling. Think back to the times that you had either traumatic experience or substantial pain and heartache that has led to the creation of some strong beliefs you still hold true to this day. Some parents report instances of extreme happiness and fulfillment with their parents that has led to them doubling down on taking these same approaches with their children now. These experiences shape our ability to identify ways in which we can connect, or we can help our kids avoid pain.

Take out a notepad, journal, or blank piece of paper and jot down some ideas and points of reference that come to mind when you think about these strong experiences that have shaped you.

- How have they affected your interactions with your child?

- Had they led to you becoming overbearing or controlling in order to help them avoid pain?
- Has this led to you trying to double down on getting them to try experiences that you found fulfilling as a child and that you have fond memories of?
- Were there ever any instances of you being bullied or assaulted by peers?
- When you were younger, did you have low self-esteem and struggle with being motivated to complete schoolwork? Has this led to you being overly critical or hyper functioning in regard to your child's schoolwork? Has this led to you backing off their schoolwork to a degree that they are now falling behind?

Take some time to really dig into this section as I find this to be extremely helpful and useful with all the parents that I work with.

Roles within Family of Origin

Next, we're going to start by talking about your own role in your own family and how it could have a significant impact on your parenting. We all take on a role within our own family of origin as we need to fit into the larger system of the family. These roles allow us to get our needs met and feel as though we are contributing to the overall dynamic in some meaningful way. We are going to go over some roles I commonly see and let's identify if they connect with you in some way.

Parentified

The first role we will look at are people who may have been *parentified*. Parentification is where the child is made to be more responsible than their parent, emotionally and physically, in areas that are not appropriate for a child to be responsible. Some ways in which this happens is if the parent is significantly abusing substances. Alcoholism and drug abuse can create a substantial amount of mistrust and anxiety in kids who are unable to rely on their parents to care for the well-being of family members, let alone themselves. The parent may also have financial struggles, and in extreme cases, leading to homelessness or utilities being shut off. They also tend to be a significant source of support for their parents, emotionally and physically, because the parent is stuck in adolescence or trying to overcome their own problems of the past. The most common and insidious ways in which this can occur is when the parent has trouble managing their time and priorities; i.e. constantly running late, forgetting items of importance, falling behind on meals or getting ready to go to an event, etc.

Children who tend to be parentified also can be emotionally responsible in ways for their parents processing their own pain and troubles within their marriage or their family of origin. They can be brought into conflicts to mediate and may also be sought out to help the parent problem solve. If their parents are fighting or possibly teetering on divorce, the kids may take on being an emotional support and processor for a parent. They may even get involved in the conflicts based on how they may see one parent being treated unfairly or inappropriately by the other. Examples of this could include a parent who is physically or emotionally abusive towards the other. The parent who is left emotionally or physically hurt may then be constantly tended to and nurtured by the child, resulting in parentification. Shame and guilt can also result in ploys to manipulate children into being emotionally responsible for their parents by complying with their requests or needs.

This can lead to parenting in the future that can come across condescending or controlling within the new family dynamic. Sometimes it can also come off as trying to be protective or trying to prevent problems from happening within the family structure due to the anxiety they experienced when they were kids. They can also be overriding decisions of one parent over the other, or overriding decisions of the child because they "know better" than others do. This can contribute to power struggles and a substantial amount of anxiety and conflict within family systems, resulting in behavioral and emotional symptoms in children and adolescents.

Spousified

The next role is *spousified*. This is when the child is placed in the position of being a partner or spouse. These duties require you to be emotionally present for the parent to process their own feelings, as if you're a sounding board for your parent(s). They tend to be on equal grounds with the parent and can make decisions that spouses would make together. They can also process adult problems and their opinions will be taken seriously. Such conversations revolve around the parent's struggles at work or interpersonally with friends, leading to the child being a pseudo therapist. These children are similar to parentified parents, but may be less pushy when it comes to decision making. They can be passive aggressive with others when others make decisions that they disagree with or think are poor ideas. They can struggle with boundaries as much as parentified children because of the unhealthy dynamic.

This is usually more the case emotionally and less physically, as parentified kids tend to be more hands on and feel more pressure to provide. Spousified kids tend to feel more as if they are an equal and that their input and decisions are there to be emotionally and physically supportive, but not dependent to the functioning or well-being of the parent or the family as a whole.

Scapegoat

The next role is the *scapegoat*. Children that are placed in the scapegoat role are the ones that take on all the emotional baggage and blame for the problems within the family. Here's a great example: think of Kevin McCallister from *Home Alone*. He was always being blamed within the family dynamic as the troublemaker amongst the relationships inside the family. No matter how he attempted to be a part of the family dynamic, he was always placed in the role of having others' frustrations taken out on.

Not just parents contribute to this role, siblings and external family members may also recognize this pattern and jump on the bandwagon. The child feels totally emotionally and physically responsible for areas of others' lives that are significantly inappropriate and unrealistic. They believe that a substantial amount of their presence and existence is a burden, or that they are unlovable. They can have significant insecurity within relationships and may try to overcompensate for problems when they occur. They can become either angry when they are being blamed or accused of doing something that is hurtful or mean, or overcompensate and take on solving the problem. They may struggle with managing their anger or become very enmeshed with others who can manipulate their emotions for personal gain.

Responsible One

Another possible role is the *responsible one*. Children placed in this role tend to be very self-sufficient. They tend to solve problems for the family before they actually occur and are constantly looking ahead to avoid problems from occurring. They very quickly take on responsibilities and roles at a young age. They can grow up to continue this role, leading them to extreme financial success, or causing them to take on roles of leadership. This can however be taken too far, as they can then be isolated from relationships or overly enmeshed in being responsible for others. These boundaries can exacerbate connection difficulties or create conflicts due to their rigid ways of thinking and actions. They also may over function for others, leading their children to be more and more helpless and incompetent. They take pride in finding solutions, but fail to recognize how they may strip others of their ability to think for themselves.

Responsible children can also be easily led to feel emotionally guilty and ashamed of their own needs as they are always having their pride placed on being helpful and thoughtful. Thus, their own emotional integrity can become lost in others. Anytime they may try and individuate, they can have feelings of shame or guilt for the lost opportunity to assist others.

Golden Child

Another role is the *golden child*. These children can essentially do no wrong and can be exorbitantly entitled and enabled. They tend to have massive emotional and physical support, regardless of their behavior, and can be emboldened to take more and more risks. They tend to be seen as the perfect son or daughter and tend to have very little recourse for wrongdoing, leading to limited self-reflection skills. Golden children also are seen as superior above all the other siblings and can receive special treatment and get perks and privileges that the other children do not. This can lead to the child becoming insecure in taking feedback or facing negative criticism from others when they are older. They can also struggle with being able to accept that they could have made a mistake or hurt someone's feelings negatively. They judge their outcomes based on their intentions instead of the impact it can have on others.

When it comes to golden children, they may have kids that are very similar to them, but also if they have challenging kids, they can lack the ability to understand or relate to them. They can also feel superior in their parenting approach, leading to potential overconfidence or underdelivering on setting limits and consequences, largely because they never required any difficult lines or consequences growing up. They can also focus too much on elevating their child's self-esteem as they feel as though the reason that they were behaving was because their sense of self was respected and valued.

Pariah/Black Sheep

The final role we'll explore is the *pariah*. This person is made to feel as though they are essentially a social-emotional outcast to most of the family. They do not fit the norms or culture of the family and struggle with acclimating effectively into the dynamic due to their interests or personality. Many children that feel this way can go in multiple directions and either thrive very well, or it can also lead to significant mental health concerns. They may have little to no connection with their family of origin and struggle with getting or giving validation and emotionally understanding to others. They may also struggle with having empathy or compassion based on not receiving this or they may have the opposite extreme. These individuals can struggle with trusting others and can have high conflict with people.

Think about these roles and how these dynamics may fit either you or your partner. You may also see these roles in family members in your family of origin, resulting in them having a major impact on you and your identity now. Take the time to reflect and write out how this could have an influence on your approach presently. If none of these fit, think about other siblings and if they had any of these roles within the family. Have they negatively impacted you and your sense of self because they had these roles? Has this impacted your beliefs in some way that could be contributing to how you are engaging with your child? Use the space below to reflect and answer these questions.

Family Culture and Cultural Impacts

Thinking again about your own upbringing, we will look at the culture that your family embraced when you were growing up.

Family culture is substantially important to values, traditions, and how love is shown.

- Did your family members emigrate from another country?
- In the culture in which you come from, is it very patriarchal or matriarchal?
- Did women or men have more respect?
- Are they viewed equally?
- Did gender roles have an impact on who did what in your household?

Culture plays a major role in shaping our beliefs and approaches to resolving conflicts within relationships. Some cultures also have emotionally enmeshed and unhealthy individual boundaries as the norm, depending on socialized beliefs and economies. In some cases, culture can create or foster emotional detachment and significant authoritarian parenting strategies. How do you think your culture has shaped the emotional closeness or distance with your child? Did it have an emotional impact on how close you were or were not to family members growing up?

Parent Projections of Others

There are times when parents I am working with will actually state that their child reminds them of somebody that they grew up with. This is a form of projection; meaning it may lead parents to respond and react to their child as if it were the person they are reminded of. It is completely unconscious in most cases. Projection can result in parents being critical or controlling with a child when it is not appropriate to the current situation. It can also lead to overly critical or judgmental responses that are inappropriate or hurtful to the parent-child relationship.

When I ask parents about this during sessions, they can make connections rather quickly, as their child may look or act very similar in their mannerisms and responses. Some cases may include family members who are drug addicts, families where one of their siblings committed suicide, or flashbacks for PTSD symptoms from physical aggression and/or sexual abuse from somebody when they were younger.

The most common situation where I encounter projection is when a sibling of a parent may currently have problems with being independent as an adult. This anxiety and concerns about their child developing into the same dysfunctional adult creates tension, conflict, and major power struggles. It would be wise to seek some level of professional help if this is the case, as this can only make matters worse if it is not processed and differentiated.

Guilt and Shame

Some cultures may use shame and guilt to motivate or change behavior. Did you grow up being guilted and shamed into compliance? These two emotional strategies are absolutely destructive towards emotional connection and the well-being of raising a child to successfully individuate. I cannot emphasize this enough. Shame and guilt, as a means to create change in any child, is unhealthy and severely emotionally confusing. It can lead to the child struggling to be able to understand who they are as an individual and feel confident in taking risks.

These emotions give the impression that they are trapped having to choose between loving others over their own individuality and sense of self expression. If you have experienced this as a child, you know how much this has a profound impact on your sense of self-worth. If you have not, I recommend that you do <u>*not adopt*</u> this strategy. It creates unhealthy emotional boundaries which can lead to significant mental health symptoms. This strategy has been profoundly used by previous generations as a main tool to gain compliance and get people to not argue or create tension. Many parents I have worked with have said that they remember significantly having their parents use guilt or shame to get control of their behavior. You may be able to relate to this.

Guilt and shame also have a way of kids becoming people pleasers and peacekeepers at the expense of themselves. This leads to a life where they can begin to believe and feel as though they will never be worthy enough of taking time, resources, or energy for themselves. They feel an extreme responsibility towards others to a degree that can create emotional enmeshment. These individually can also go in the opposite direction of becoming extremely cold and manipulative to also get their way. They can believe that because they had to endure this level of treatment from their parents and it "worked well", why not implement it now? This is a form of destructive entitlement that can then create a rigid belief around a strategy or set of strategies that are deeply unhelpful.

Emotional enmeshment and healthy relationship boundaries:

Can you relate to this? Parents I have worked with remember the adage of being seen, not heard. Was this how you were raised as well, to be seen and not heard? The difference with today's generation of children is that they are seen, heard, validated, understood, and given more emotional expression than at any time in history. This paradigm shift is based on the parents trying to give their children the opposite of their experience. Of course, some parents are still embracing the same strategies that are antiquated and outdated for today's standards of treating children. So, we are seeing both sides of the spectrum here, and this can pose some confusion, as there are so many differing opinions. However, too much of anything, even something as positive as love can become toxic and too much.

A healthy boundary between a parent and child is one that allows the child to be themselves and grow into themselves through successes and failures they create, while the parent is encouraging and supportive, holding them accountable to learning to be more self-sufficient over time. Please note that nowhere in this definition is there physical support to get the child to succeed or fail. This is critical to recognize, as most parents I work with had no emotional support and limited physical support when they were a child, and now they are going in the opposite direction of providing too much emotional support and way too much physical support.

Lastly, if you are living by the saying, "A parent is only as happy as their least happy child", please recognize that this in its essence is emotional enmeshment. The parents' and child's emotions are one, and this can unintentionally place a lot of pressure on your child or worse, put more pressure on you to enable and lead them to believe that they are incapable…more on this to come.

I am going to address boundaries more in depth in future chapters, too.

Food for thought:

Emotional Support Definition: Processing feelings and perspectives in a way that is open minded and validating the child both verbally and physically. (Hugging, giving them kisses, snuggling, calming them down when crying, verbal reassurance and positive affirmations, reflectively listening to their experience.

Physical Support Definition: Completing or participating in tasks that the child is capable of doing independently and learning how to manage in a self-sufficient way, but the parent still does.

- What kind of boundaries of emotional and physical support did you get when you were a child?
- Did you get a lot of emotional support from your parents? If so, how? Do you try to do the same for your kids?
- Did you get physical support? If so, how? Do you try to do the same for your kids?

Use the space here to answer these questions.

_____
_____
_____
_____
_____
_____
_____
_____
_____
_____
_____
_____
_____
_____
_____
_____
_____
_____
_____
_____
_____
_____
_____
_____

Take some time to really reflect on these questions. Take into consideration how your family's boundaries have influenced you.

Chapter 3

YOUR OWN SH*T NOW...

Enough Freudian mumbo jumbo, let's dig into more present stuff that's contributing to that shitty parenting approach. At the end of this chapter you will be able to…

1. recognize your own personal issues that need to be addressed to be less shitty.
2. see how your in-laws or own parents may be getting in the way of progress.
3. make sure new partners are not influencing or engaging in parenting responsibilities and when it is appropriate to integrate them into parenting.
4. realize how important your marriage is over your children.
5. put more of your own needs first to stop narcissism in your kids.
6. identify places to get help individually if you need it.

7. have a clear action plan of steps to roll out in order to be more self aware in your interactions.

Additional Parenting Figures

To effectively balance work and family, other supports such as parents, in-laws, siblings, or friends are often utilized. When you are around these individuals do you notice specific changes in your approach, or do you defer to them to assist in parenting responsibilities? If so, are you including them in this parenting process? I would highly recommend that you utilize support and people that are going to be encouraging you to be a better parent, but are not going to overstep their boundaries and take control for you. It is important to make sure that grandparents recognize their place in the family system. Unfortunately, they like to remind you about how things used to be "back in their day". Make it clear that the only people making parenting decisions should be you and your co-parent. They may be the ones making you more of a shitty parent than you already are.

In-laws and over functioning grandparents can be exceptionally triggering to parents. A lot of clients fall into patterns of trying to over function and enable their kids because they do not want the criticism and judgment from their parents, similar to that in which they grew up experiencing. Some may also be triggered to be more people pleasing and give into parenting approaches that your parents or in-laws utilized as you do not want to create conflict. Welp, guess what?! I say now is the time to put them in their place! It's time to establish the boundaries that you more than likely needed then and are desperately trying to create now. Let's face it! They are more than likely going to judge you even if you follow their advice to a T anyways!

New partner?

If you have a new partner after a separation, are you including them in this process? Boyfriends and girlfriends <u>SHOULD NOT</u> be participating in any parenting activities or functions. If this is currently happening, please make sure that it ends. You should include new partners in parenting responsibilities only once you have established a long-term committed relationship with the person (relationship lasting more than 6 months exclusively) and you have moved in together. Bringing someone into this role should also be deeply reflected on as they are going to now model a substantial amount for the child to carry with them into adulthood. These individuals should be role models and should have both the ability to be emotionally and physically supportive. They should also respect the biological parents' requests and take a backseat role in parenting. It is inappropriate based on the role that they should be playing in your child's life. Please share with them the steps you are taking to be a less shitty parent. Feel free to share any materials and talk with them about some of the new ways in which you're learning about throughout this book.

If you have a new marriage and are having them enter into the parenting space, you should absolutely include them in reading this book. You should also discuss their feelings and perspectives on what makes parenting successful and how their upbringing has shaped their feelings and perspectives on how to engage in raising kids. I would highly recommend that if they are going to enter into the parenting realm, they should absolutely focus more on building rapport than any other skill I outline in this book. This will allow the new parenting figure to build trust, influence, and show that they are genuinely interested in emotionally connecting with the child. They need to focus on building a bond and connection before even considering establishing a limit, boundary, or consequence. I would highly recommend that they be more of an emotional support and processor while the biological parents are the ones establishing the firmer limits, boundaries and consequences all kids need in order to remain below the parental hierarchy.

Marriage Prioritization

This is one of the most important areas to cover because it can substantially influence your family dynamic. You and your partner's marriage may be a major source of conflict, which is well known to exacerbate and create behavioral problems in children. It is hard to identify and differentiate between whether the child's behavior and parenting conflicts are the core source of marital problems or if other factors are contributing to marital discord. I always assume that it is both to cover all my bases and you should too. I recommend that you make sure that you get this area under control. You're already shitty so no need to make yourself shittier!

It's vital to improve the problems you and your spouse may be having in order to effectively address the concerns you are having with your child. I have worked with many children whose parents are divorced. Sadly, one of the main ways they could have stayed married, is if they had placed more prioritization on their relationship and deprioritized their kids and the problems the kids were facing. A lot of times more attention and engagement leads to making the problems worse instead of better. Putting prioritization on you and your partner has the potential to be more positive than negative for the emotional well-being of your child as this also highlights that the hierarchy of the family is something that is incredibly important and essential to them and creates respect of both you and your co-parent.

Some parents have really had a difficult time embracing this concept, as societally it is not accepted well. Remember how the village has gone dark…well, here is a great example. I professionally recommend that at the very least, you create some balance of equality between your relationship with your spouse and your children to be less shitty. You may be shocked at how much you are not always talking about problems and engaging in problem dialogue with your partner can drastically improve the situation and the child taking on more responsibility since they are not getting as much attention around their shenanigans.

I know that you are doubting me because of all the podcasts, well intentioned books you have read, and the advice from Instagram reels, but let's look at some positives of making your marriage a priority.

First, by prioritizing your spouse, it allows your child to see that the world does not revolve around them and that their needs are not the most important.

Second, it establishes a strong parental hierarchy and differentiates the child from the parental authority.

Third, it produces a need for the child to develop more autonomy and independence. This will drastically improve self-esteem and a sense of self that will become resilient over time.

Fourth, it allows the child to also see a healthy marriage dynamic and how to create a family hierarchy. This achieves balance and boundaries that assist in creating more peace than problems.

Most importantly, it reduces the likelihood of children developing a perspective that is narcissistic or entitled. I have seen that this single step can have a profound effect on the family dynamic. I challenge you and your partner to commit to doing more together. This concept also goes for you having your own individual time, which is our next goal.

Individual Time

Matt, are you kidding me? Time for myself? Where do you expect me to find time for myself when so many people are pulling me in all different directions? I literally cannot go to the bathroom for 2 minutes before there's a knock on the door followed by "mooommmmm".

And there you have it, that's why 'me time' is so important! We need them, your children, to start pulling themselves in their own directions. Obviously, this is limited if you have small children and I know that in today's busy world it is hard to do this. I promise, though, this is necessary and there are ways to do it. Think about it...

- Do you currently have activities that will supersede the child's activities or needs?

- Can they miss a practice or class once a month for you to take time for yourself?
- Do you have peer relationships outside of the family home in which you do activities with?
- Do you have areas of fulfillment and connection outside of your immediate family?

If not, you may significantly run the risk of becoming emotionally enmeshed or codependent with your child. This codependence can have a significant impact on your child becoming independent and emotionally secure within themselves. By taking some time consistently for yourself it can allow your child to also do the same. This is the power of modeling. Being a good model is less shitty. You're always going to feel shitty, even when you want to take time for yourself, and I promise this modelling and time will benefit both you and your kids in the long run. So, push through and recognize that this is a normal feeling.

Get Support

It's critical to recognize that you may need additional support. Please do not hesitate to get professional help. This does not make you weak. I promise this can massively benefit you in the process of becoming the least shitty parent possible. This stress may put you in fight or flight mode. Some parents are starting recovery from substance abuse, or are struggling financially. It is understandable that these can bleed into your parenting. We all need support and have different experiences that have shaped us. Please contact your insurer to see if they have resources that are in your network.

I can highly recommend using www.psychologytoday.com in order to find a therapist that may be in your network. If you can afford it, I highly recommend looking outside of your insurance network as these individuals tend to be more experienced and have a significant caseload for a reason. Finding the right fit is also appropriate and necessary. Please seek out multiple therapists and see if they will do a phone consultation to learn more about their style and how they work. I also have resources on my website to highlight the differences in therapists based on their training and educational experience. Please go to www.westportctcounseling.com and you can find additional resources there.

We've covered a lot in this chapter. And I'm sure it may feel a bit overwhelming since I asked you to dig deep and uncover some truths you may have never thought of before. Here are some takeaways to keep in mind as we move forward on this journey.

Dos and Don'ts:

Do

- Start to be aware of the dynamics and upbringing patterns from your family of origin over the next week as you engage with your child(ren).
- Ask for support in processing your upbringing by enlisting a professional if you are recognizing that you have more pain and projection than you were previously aware of.

- Create awareness with your partner or spouse so they can also assist you in being more aware of these projections. There is no shame in getting support, especially from a loving partner.

Don'ts

- Beat yourself up through this process. Give yourself some empathy and compassion, as we are all struggling with different areas. Your kids love you and they need you to be the best you can be!
- Tell your children about these projections as they can potentially utilize these to reduce taking responsibility for their behavior later. It's also breaking a boundary to process your projections with your children!
- Use the information that you and your partner gather to be hurtful or place blame on one another. Instead be supportive and compassionate as they want to be a better parent, but may be struggling with knowing how.

Awareness is the main goal of this chapter. It may be hard to look at some of these aspects, but keep moving forward by reflecting. Talk with other supports, such as friends and family members that you are comfortable processing with. Look for people who are going to be encouraging. Enlist other parents to join you in being a less shitty parent by passing this book along and seeing if they can relate.

Chapter 4

THE INSANE POWER OF RAPPORT BUILDING

This chapter is specifically designed to help you harness the power or rapport building. Rapport is one of the great ways in which you can have influence over others. It allows you and your child to engage in a loving and connecting way, even when there are conflicts. The goal of this section is to build back connections and not focus on correction. We also want to make sure that your child feels that you are not looking for them to be perfect. You want to focus on *progression over perfection* (more on this in a future chapter).

At the end of this chapter, you will be able to…

1. understand what rapport is and is not.
2. identify areas of interest that your child has that will improve your ability to connect.

3. recognize ways you may be mixing rapport and problem solving.
4. identify areas of positive engagement to start to praise your child.
5. take ownership of missed opportunities to build rapport.
6. create dialogue to better understand more ways to build rapport.
7. recognize how hypocrisy and poor example setting contribute to limited credibility and disengagement from the child, thereby hindering rapport.
8. use the benefit of the doubt dialogue to show understanding.

The value of rapport is that it allows you to keep the relationship going in a positive and encouraging way, even when your kids make mistakes and problems arise. This emotional influence is so powerful you may not even have to use leverage. (Also going to be touching on this in future chapters).

Most parents struggle through rapport building, as they fear that they are becoming friends with their children. Some may have grown up in an environment with limited structure and expectations, or where they saw their parents as absolute authority. These experiences shape parents and teach them to steer clear of being "friendly" with their children. Throughout this section, you will see that being friends and being friendly are two very different things. Less shitty parents have rapport with their children and have successfully harnessed the power of being friendly and building a deeper emotional bond with their kids.

A bond you are definitely going to be borrowing against when problems arise.

Understanding and Utilizing Rapport

We want to utilize all the opportunities we have with our kids to build them up. ESP is founded in building a connection with your child that will allow you to have influence and establish authority. The main reason that rapport is not more widely used is most parents never experienced it when they were young. Rapport is the ability to attune to others' emotional priorities and needs to share in strong emotional experiences and connect harmoniously. As I mentioned before, some parents have confused this with being a friend to their child. They fear that this will ultimately create an unhealthy dynamic and give their child the impression that they are on the same level. The intention is not to become friends with your child, but you should be interested in them with sincerity.

To clarify, rapport is…

- focused on emotional content and areas of interest that _only the person you are talking to care or have insight on_.
- _emotionally positive, encouraging, or seek further knowledge of these areas of interest._
- showing _curiosity and asking questions to build off_. It gives the person the ability to further share or talk about their areas of interest.
- always requiring _active listening and validation._

- focused on _stacking and building off previous rapport questions_ and interactions. _Shows consistency and thoughtfulness._

Rapport is NOT...

- focused on emotional content and areas of interest that _you share with the person you are talking to or may care or have insight on_. Gives the impression you are only talking with them to talk about yourself.
- areas that _you think they should, could, or might have interest in_ if they only tried or looked into it.
- trying to share the conversation or _talk about areas you care about or what you can expand upon_ in their area of interest. Shows that you may want to brag or show off.
- _major or minor insight giving or sharing_, unless the person is asking or requesting the engagement from you. _Comes across condescending and inconsiderate._
  - IF they do ask, though, it should be kept short and lead to further insight questioning or building.

Uncovering Your Child's Areas of Interest

Most of the parents believe that they have better rapport with their children than they really do. Generally, shitty parents try to build rapport in areas that they are well versed or care a lot about. This is a critical mistake as it sets the parent up to fall into the role of teacher. Instead, parents need to become more of an active listener and validator.

A STEP-BY-STEP PROCESS ON HOW TO BE A LESS SH!TTY PARENT

Remember the goal is connection, not correction.

Here are some ideas of areas that your child may have interest and engagement around that you can utilize in order to build rapport with them.

- Video games
- Movies
- Specific sports teams
- Clothing
- Specific Music (Yes, even rap music)
- Art/Photography
- Makeup/Hair/Nails
- Videos on internet or Youtubers they follow
- Memes/Funny Videos on internet
- Social Media Influencers
- Books/Comics/Magazines
- Specific toys that they play with constantly
- School subjects they enjoy
- Close friendships and peers they enjoy
- Technology
- Any activity that they enjoy or engage in

Do you remember when Fortnite the video game came out? Parents at the time were largely opposed to their children playing this and would attempt to limit the time spent on the game, with little success and much push back. Would you be shocked to know that this was in fact a time for parents to build rapport as a means to eventually limit their behavior (their gaming)? Parents were given an opportunity through the game, to step into the world of Fortnite and show enthusiasm around something their child truly enjoyed. The idea being, if parents want to establish authority and eventually get their children off the video game, they must first show interest in what they are playing. They need to feel as though you understand and comprehend what and how they go about enjoying it. It allows you to validate their experience and use it as leverage to talk about principles. Don't worry, we will talk more about this next chapter.

Mixing Rapport with Problem Solving

There is a reason you only need to focus right now on building rapport. It builds authenticity and lowers the defenses of the child. Kids often feel like their parents are being fake or are trying to trick them into compliance. There is research to suggest that for every 5 positive interactions with someone, it null's 1 negative interaction. This means, you will need 5 interactions of building rapport for every 1 challenge you give the child. How do you think you currently stack up with that ratio?

An example of mixing rapport building and problem solving happens when parents only show interest in an area right before they have to challenge the child. A parent may say something like…

"Hey, how is your video game going?" (The kid responds.) "Oh, that's great I am glad it is going well. I need you to stop though and come clean up your dishes from the table. We are working on cleanliness, and you left them out."

You can feel how this is coercive. In order to build rapport, you must set some time aside each day to engage with your child for 5-15 minutes. The ONLY GOAL in that time is to build rapport—be encouraging, enthusiastic, ask questions, DO NOT "Parent". This is a huge investment for such a small period of time. If you are responding right now with, I don't even have that time, you may want to look at your prioritization, as this could be affecting your credibility with your child. You may also want to supplement giving them a hard time in the area and instead using it to get to know them more.

Highlighting the Positive Elements of Your Child's Behavior

Highlighting positive behavior is often an area that shitty parents struggle to implement consistently. This can be difficult because the child may be consistently so deregulated that it is hard to find areas that they are doing well. However, if you seek to find the positive you will. Our minds have a way of confirming a bias that we already have, which is called confirmation bias. When we have a strong belief, we seek out only the evidence to support that belief. In the interest of building rapport, start to challenge your bias and seek out different (positive) bias.

What aspects of their life are your kids currently doing well in? Highlight these and start to make mention of them in real time with them. They need to feel as though they are being valued and appreciated for the ways they have already made progress in learning. When you recognize this happening, you may want to praise and highlight the principle. An example may be, "I see that you were able to help your sister out earlier pick up her toys. You should feel proud of yourself for being supportive and helpful."

We want them further working towards embracing these principles instead of feeling as though they can do nothing well. We do not want your child to feel as if they can do nothing well. If your child already feels this way, we need to undo some negative beliefs as they may have a perspective of learned helplessness. That is where they adapt to having a belief that they are powerless to their situation and therefore give into negative coping strategies, as attempting to do well is unachievable.

Accept Responsibility for Past Limited Rapport Building

Apologizing and taking responsibility for limited rapport building has a profound healing power for the relationship with your child. It validates the emotions of the child and will drastically reduce the ways in which you struggle to create a connection. The child usually responds by lowering defenses over time and/or lowering their reactivity to you almost immediately. Below is an example of how a conversation like this could go.

"Hey, I am realizing that in the past I would try to engage with you in areas that I really only had an interest in or at least we had a shared interest in. I am recognizing that this probably makes you feel at times I am only interested in serious topics like school and your (insert extracurricular activity). I want to start to engage with you around areas you find interesting and that you enjoy. I may start asking you about these topics and I hope you are willing to give me a chance. I don't want to be annoying, and

I don't want to be overbearing, but I do want you to know I want to improve our relationship."

This not only allows the child to feel that you are more self-aware, but it also takes off some of the past blame or guilt that they could have had in conflicts with you. It validates their feeling and need for connection with you. Also, it is appropriate modeling to recognize when you have made a mistake. In turn, this hopefully will allow the child to do the same over time.

Ask for Insight on How You Can Further Improve the Relationship

Don't be afraid to ask for some feedback from your kid! Believe it or not, they will tell you exactly what they have wanted or needed from you. Literally! They are constantly testing you and merely asking them for advice can have a a major impact on them feeling respected. Obviously, they will always throw around some silly ideas (Video game console, new phone, vacation to Tahiti [literally happened in a case I worked on], car, etc.). Clarify that what you are asking for is more about emotional support or engagement, not physical/tangible resources.

PLEASE DO YOUR BEST TO MAKE EDUCATED GUESSES FIRST— if not this can come across as lazy. I have heard from kids I work with that this seems disingenuous. Without seeing your own effort first, children may also feel as though you are putting more responsibility on them to better the relationship than you are on yourself. It is also helpful to utilize others who already seem to have rapport with them. Start to embrace some of the ways in which they engage in being friendly and encouraging towards your child. Simply replicating some of their approaches and being consistent with them can have a positive impact. Identify how they approach the child with their body language and tonality. These two factors contribute to over 93% of communication. 7% is the actual percentage of spoken words.

Hypocrisy and Credibility Concerns

Professionals often hear from children that they "don't respect their parents" because they are hypocritical or set poor examples. YOU DO NOT WANT TO OPERATE UNDER THE ADAGE, "Do as I say, not as I do". This leads to kids having little respect for their parents. You can implement all the rapport building in the world, but if you operate from this perspective, you will fail and struggle.

Operating with this mentality makes it appears a though you may have entitlement to more flexibility than they do. This belief infuriates children as it makes them feel as if they must abide by some strict code you have "made up".

Second, it leads them to believe that you are not credible in your actions so how can you be credible with your knowledge? They will doubt anything that you have to say, and therefore any parenting approach you take will fail.

It is vitally important that you reflect and live by the same principles you are trying to instill in your children. Take the steps to start to show improvement and consistency in these areas as the child will see you learning and taking more responsibility. This is yet another opportunity for you to model taking responsibility and hopefully they will incorporate this same approach.

Please remember I am focused on you not only enhancing your child's behavior, but the entire family's. If you have an unwilling spouse or co-parent that you are attempting to work with in this area, this can be extremely frustrating for you. It is acceptable and reasonable to validate this frustration of credibility with your child. This will only backfire on you and your credibility as well. It is their responsibility to manage their behavior and if they are choosing not to, do not minimize your child for having this experience. Some believe that this is not an appropriate approach as you do not want to minimize or put down the other parent. I agree that you should not intentionally go out of your way to do this, but if the child is bringing this to your attention you have to validate it. It will also minimize your credibility with your child if you disregard your co-parent's behavior as well.

Use Benefit of the Doubt Dialogue

Before you challenge anyone, ever, in any relationship, they need to believe that you think that they are a good person. If they do not believe this about your perspective, anything that comes out of your mouth, no matter how "right" or "accurate" it is, will be minimized immediately. We all need to feel that the people we love believe we are inherently good.

Benefit of the doubt allows you to soften the blow when you have to criticize or challenge others. This gives them the impression that you understand that other influences are having an impact on their decision making and behavior. <u>It does not mean that you excuse the behavior.</u> I will talk further about this process in the following chapter on how to validate, not accommodate.

So, let's look at a process to actually implement. Let's say that the child is not getting their homework completed in a timely manner (principle would be time management). Benefit of the doubt would be something along the lines of this, "I can understand that your homework is boring. I also get that you are burnt out after going to school all day. I don't blame you for taking some time after school to unwind. You will definitely be able to manage your time effectively so that you can get it done at an appropriate time." See how the entirety of this dialogue is positive and focused on giving the child understanding of their perspective. We DO NOT justify or excuse the behavior.

Please keep in mind this strategy doesn't just work well with kids, it works well with all people. You may want to try this with all family members in order to create more emotional closeness and connection. This also helps keep friction to a minimum in future instances of tension, as you will have been laying the foundation that you believe they are well intentioned.

Now I am not naive and believe that this is going to get your kids to follow through on this. The goal of this is so that when they DO NOT do it, you can focus on troubleshooting and getting them to reflect on their choices in order to find their own solution in the future. I will go over more about this later on in the book as we will talk about using consequences more strategically.

Joking and Teasing. TERRIBLE IDEAS!

Another area in which parents believe they are building rapport, but they truly could be destroying it, are jokes. Some parents believe that teasing and poking fun at the child is a positive rapport building activity. They think that this playfulness of messing with the child also allows them to have thick skin as they get older and not take negative comments very personally. However, it is a destructive strategy.

The role of a parent is to be a supporter and positive influence on children's perspective and beliefs, especially about themselves. ALWAYS. Teasing and playing around by joking about their behavior or mannerisms can have a long-term negative effect on the child's beliefs about themselves. Please follow the old adage, "If you don't have anything nice to say, don't say anything at all."

Complimenting and recognizing positive things about the child may be deeply uncomfortable for some parents. Some didn't receive this at all when they were growing up, so now it feels uncomfortable to do it on their own. You may want to practice complimenting yourself to start. You can also benefit from this strategy as it will further empower you and make you feel substantially less insecure around your less shitty parenting approach. Practicing the benefit of the doubt strategies is a great middle ground to start.

Dos and Don'ts

So, let's go over the dos and don'ts of this chapter so you can take clear action steps.

Do

- start to use the benefit of the doubt dialogue to improve credibility with all family members.
- identify positive compliments you can give children—and yourself. Look to change your bias.
- recognize principles that you may be hypocritical about and start to work on improving them.
- engage with them in areas of interest that only they enjoy, instead of mixed areas.
- ask for feedback from the child and others <u>AFTER</u> making educated guesses and efforts on ways to build better rapport.
- sit down and talk with the child about past and present behaviors that resulted in them not being close with you.

Don't

- tease or poke fun at the child from this point forward, even after you have built rapport with them.
- continue to confirm biases that are only leading to you focusing on negative aspects of the child's behavior.
- ignore feedback from others

- dismiss your responsibility in conflicts and blame the child for lost opportunities in the past to build rapport.

Remember this is going to take some time for you to accilmate to. Some of you learning this had very limited emotional rapport built into your family dynamic. Some of you may even recognize you had all the negative aspects just outlined in this module. Sadly, not all are uncommon either. This is your chance now to redefine this for yourself and your child. It allows you the ability to know exactly how to improve on this so you can start being less shitty.

Chapter 5

COMPLIANCE/PROBLEMS VS PRINCIPLES/ACCOUNTABILITY

Time to end the arguing over details and semantics! That's right, I am going to help you have strategies by the end of this chapter on how to stop the nonsensical arguing that only infuriates your kids, exhausts you, and leads to a death spiral of nowhere!

At the end of this chapter, you will be able to...

1. recognize the major differences between compliance and accountability.
2. realize how shitty you have been for looking only at the behavior.
3. pivot from talking about problems and instead focusing on principles

4. realize the power of principles being about learning instead of the child being bad.
5. give healthy control and freedom to your kids in order to not micromanage.
6. not fall into arguing details and semantics with your Yale trained lawyer kids.
7. learn how to use validation to stop you from accommodating your little lawyers.
8. identify your specific principles so you can shift your dialogue to feel less shitty.

During this chapter, we are going to go over a radically different way of thinking about parenting. Shitty parents focus on compliance, whereas less shitty parents focus on accountability.

Focusing on accountability is what is going to help get you out of a shitty job of micromanaging and back into a position as a less shitty parent. Reestablish your rightful and healthy place in the parental hierarchy.

The first thing you want to do in an accountability-based approach is to begin to slowly but surely DISTANCE yourself from the child's decision making. I'm not talking about distancing yourself from your child–just distancing yourself from their decision-making process so that they can begin to learn to think for themselves.

We want a sustainable long-term approach to your child's development. When they get into the adult world there is no one there to hold their hand and manage them. Poor choices have consequences and good choices have benefits. Their ability to make decisions will determine whether they thrive or struggle as an adult. If this does NOT happen, they can start to internalize all negative outcomes and create learned helplessness or a victim mentality. Both of which, I promise, you do not want your child to have to unlearn when they become bigger, stronger, and more intelligent on how to manipulate.

If a child learns to take responsibility for the process of making decisions, it improves the likelihood that they will make good decisions and gives them the best chance of being independent and self-sufficient as they grow up. Most importantly, we want them to be free thinkers who won't get taken advantage of and are best positioned for success in life. Lastly, no one likes a cellar dweller... you know the kids that live in the basement rent free, playing video games, smoking weed, and leeching resources because they struggle with stress tolerance? You know what I'm talking about.

This is the less shitty shift I want you to start making today–from a compliance-based approach to an approach that focuses on accountability. It's exactly like the parable of "Teaching a person to fish rather than just giving them a fish." One day you're not going to be there for them every day, and you want them to be able to fish on their own.

That's accountability. But so what? What are they going to be held accountable for? And that's the next thing we're going to talk about: Success Principles.

Successful parents are focused on instilling principles over problems. The definition of instill in the Oxford dictionary is, "gradually but firmly establish (an idea or attitude, especially a desirable one) in a person's mind."

A reward approach, accommodating approach or compliance-based approach are all about managing behaviors. In an accountability-based approach, I talk about instilling principles.

Here are a couple of examples:

A behavior you might want to correct is your child running in the house and dropping their shoes, jacket and backpack on the floor by the front door. What we want the child to learn is the principle—which is picking up after oneself for the benefit of everyone who lives in the house. You would also want them to learn to be considerate, especially if that behavior of not being considerate of others shows up in another scenario.

Another example may be the behavior of a teen who comes home late from curfew or a child who is late getting in the car in the morning. Both fall under the principles of being proactive or time management.

I like to think of principles as umbrellas—each umbrella stem is the principle (like cleanliness, for example) that covers a multitude of different problematic behaviors and scenarios that you find yourself in with your kids. They struggle to keep their room clean, they don't pick up their trash off the coffee table, they leave stuff in your car, and even leave wet towels on your hardwood floors! If we teach the child the principle, then they can start making the connection with these individual behaviors, and we eventually don't have to micromanage their behavior on a daily basis in each of these scenarios.

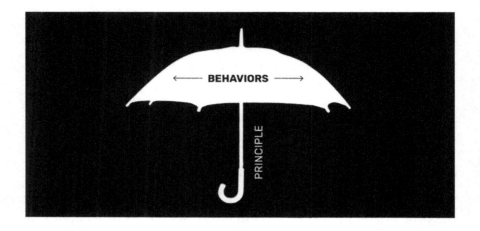

I know you're already asking, "Well, Matt, that sounds great and all, but my kids are animals! How are we going to make them accountable for these principles?" And we're going to talk about other concepts, which include developing rapport and implementing consequences in a moment. But for now, I really want to make sure you understand how important this part is. We're going to shift our thinking from talking about behaviors to talking about principles. I tell parents to recite the mantra "principles over problems."

First thing–it's no longer going to be about the current problem. If we are constantly talking about the current problem— the shoes, the backpack, shoving their sister, their cell phone, etc., it devolves into nagging which is simply micromanaging, also known as, shitty parenting. This has a way of stripping a person's pride and dignity. You may have experienced a micromanager at work–it's absolutely draining to work for someone like this and you feel like you're held hostage to their daily demands.

When we micromanage our children, they lose a sense of autonomy and they will PUSH BACK at you to try and regain it. And this is where you get the conflict, the endless arguments and the lack of compliance and co-operation. Also, think about how they may also think that this dynamic is appropriate because they are not good enough or incapable of thinking for themselves. This process could lead to future relationships where they may get taken advantage of or tolerating treatment that could be abusive. I know this seems like a stretch, but trust me, I have seen it in my older clients when we look into their family of origin dynamics. Back to the principles…

The broader the principle, or bigger the umbrella, the better. If we have fewer, bigger principles, it's easier for the child to learn and understand. Think of a golf umbrella that covers a lot of content instead of 2 travel umbrellas that could overlap based on the problems and scenarios you are addressing with your kids.

The best part about principles is that it's harder to argue about a principle than a behavior or problem.

If you talk about the backpack, the kid can always come up with an excuse. "I was in a hurry, it won't happen again". Except that it will happen again because he or she hasn't bought into the principle.

If you talk about keeping things tidy, organized or discuss cleanliness, it's much harder to argue with that. Who wants to live in a messy house where we don't take care of our stuff and have to trip over things when we come in the front door? That's harder to argue–they'll try to argue it, because that's what they do, but it's MUCH harder for them. If they do try this, which I promise you they will, you can say something along the lines of, "All of that may be true, and yet we are focusing on the principle of (insert principle here)." Got ya, Timmy! Mom's outsmarted you now!!!

If you talk about principles, you won't get caught up in arguing details. The details are what your child currently understands, and we want to elevate the conversation beyond that so they can start developing awareness of the "recurring problems", rather than the "current problem".

If you arm your child with principles, it helps them understand what you are actually trying to teach them. It's not about their coat, their backpack, their shoes—it's about keeping your living space tidy and organized. Kids also really latch onto bigger ideas better than the details.

Have you ever got caught in a conversation with your child with endless "Whys"? You've been there, right? It's a losing strategy—they just keep asking why, and then it becomes a war of attrition and you run out of answers.

"Timmy, I really don't know why toilet paper is on a roll instead of in a box. Go ask your father…"

If you talk about principles, we go straight to the biggest WHY—straight to the answer. "Why don't I want the backpack and the shoes by the front door? It's about CLEANLINESS, which we've already discussed many times. So I don't trip over them when I come in. So we can actually open the front door without moving your stuff out of the way."

Principles allow you to talk about what you want rather than what you don't want. It's a more positive discussion. It's focused on what you're trying to achieve as opposed to what you're trying to avoid.

Think of it this way: when you go to a restaurant, you don't tell the waiter or the waitress what you don't want for dinner. "I don't want the fish tacos and I don't want the Cobb salad."

"Well, then what do you want?" Right?

Your kid is the confused waiter or waitress in this scenario. They're just like: "So what is it that you want for dinner?" and you're just saying, "not this and not that." Less shitty parents tell them what you want—what you want is the principle—again, which might be cleanliness, a neat and tidy household, or whatever.

If you focus on principles, you're not going to be micromanaging them anymore. You're not going to be arguing over the minutiae, semantics and nonsense. The child is less likely to feel picked on and nagged. If they feel nagged, they can become spiteful, vindictive and argumentative. The reason they push back is that they want control. Talking about principles rather than behavior gives them some control and autonomy.

Who doesn't want autonomy? We all value freedom and independence.

If children can focus on the principles, they can start to look at their own behavior in the context of that principle and see the recurring patterns. You're actually arming them with useful information and teaching them to make decisions in the context of principles and goals you're trying to achieve.

They are forced to put some skin in the game and take some responsibility for their decisions.

Accountability	Success Principles

- Distance yourself from child's decision-making
- Facilitate:
  » Thinking
  » Independence
  » Self-Sufficiency
	- The boarder, the better
	- Fewer principles that cover more behaviors
	- Avoid arguing details
	- Bring Awareness of recurring problem
	- Help them understand what you're actually trying to teach them

To help start making this shift, I want you to do an exercise right now. Take a blank piece of paper and write out all the problems that are causing recurring nightmares with your kids. Shoes by the front door, shoving their siblings, etc.—all those little problems that you argue about with your kids every day. And THEN, I want you to see if there are a few overarching success principles that cover most of them. For example, these might be keeping your hands to yourself, keeping the house neat and tidy, proactivity, consideration, etc. You'll likely find that there are common themes among most of them, and THESE are the principles that we should be discussing with our kids. This is an easier conversation. Trust me, your kids will also get exhausted by hearing the same principle over and over again, and they may start to mimic you stating the principle. That would be great because that means they are getting it!

So, now we're going to talk about the practical side of this. How do we implement this? What do you say to your kids when you see them doing something you don't like, or NOT doing something you want them to do?

A principles-based approach is the WHAT and the WHY. Now we're going to talk about the HOW.

This is where the emotional validation comes in.

So, your kid rushes in the door after school, takes off their shoes, jacket and backpack, drops them on the floor right at the front door and runs up the stairs before you can say anything.

You wait a second and then follow them up the stairs. "Can you please go back downstairs and put your items away."

You know the drill—here comes the explanations, excuses, and arguments. "I was in a hurry, I had to go to the bathroom, I was going to come back later and pick it up, etc". The whole thing.

Here's what I want you to say, something like this:

"No, no, no. All of that's true. It just comes back to cleanliness. I know you had to go pee. That's totally understandable. And you're still learning to embrace the principle of cleanliness, not just in this area, but in a lot of other areas. You're going to start to figure this stuff out because we're going to keep talking about cleanliness."

Instead of arguing with them, all I want you to do is agree with it. "Yeah, that's all true and just comes back to cleanliness. This is an area and this is a principle where this is an opportunity for you to start to embrace this idea more. Because dad, mom and I, whoever is obviously talking to them, we're going to keep talking about this principle because this is the answer to the test of life, we didn't make these rules up, either. By the way, this is just how life works."

I created a phrase I use with my clients that says "validate don't accommodate." This allows you to be aware of these traps where you want to accommodate your child's feelings and enable them, instead of recognizing the feeling they are having, making that reasonable, and challenging their inappropriate response by empowering them to find a better solution.

With me so far? End the argument before it even starts.

Identify YOUR Principles

Less shitty parents get to the heart of the conflict instead of arguing endlessly or lecturing your child. It leads to a reduction in arguing details to the problem, which are irrelevant and meaningless to the principles. This will also allow you and your partner to agree upon principles, so you are working in unison. Shitty parents are arguing about two different problems. One highlights the principle, while the other tends to argue the approach the parent is taking. This ultimately leads to the parents fighting and never getting to be able to use accountability for the child.

Below are examples of *principles* that will be useful when talking with your children. Please go through this and check them off to assess if these are useful based on your child(ren)'s current behavior. Be succinct and try to narrow it down to 3-4 maximum. Try and pick ones that highlight the _broadest part of a problem dynamic_ rather than being very specific. Remember the golf umbrella analogy. This allows you to keep the principles to a minimum and maximize effectiveness.

- Cleanliness
- Self-care
- Managing disappointment
- Accepting "no"
- Contribution
- Personal space/physical boundaries
- Consideration
- Proactivity
- Patience/Delayed Gratification
- Initiative
- Organization and order
- Keeping hands, body, and items to ourselves, even when we are hurting
- Understanding value/showing value for items
- Gratitude/appreciation
- Prioritization of work before play
- Mind your own business/Stay in your own lane
- Perseverance
- Time, place, and people for doing activities and humor
- Balance/Moderation
- Time Management/Structuring time and activity appropriately

Ranking System for Principle Concepts

This allows you to address them in a ranking that is strategic and more effective. Think of it this way: How can you get the child to pick up after themselves when their ability to keep their hands to themselves is far more pressing of an issue? Please start from the top and work your way down based on the ranking list below. Please feel free to add your own, just keep in mind to have them fall into this ranking.

1.) PRACTICING SAFETY TO SELF AND OTHERS

- Keeping hands to oneself
- Personal space/physical boundaries
- Self-control when we have been hurt either physically or emotionally

2.) CREATING AND MAINTAINING PERSONAL RESPONSIBILITY/PERSONAL BOUNDARIES

- Cleanliness
- Self-Care
- Accepting "no"
- Taking initiative
- Picking up after oneself
- Patience/Developing understanding of time
- Time Management
- Prioritization of working hard before playing hard

- Mind your own business/Stay in your own lane
- Perseverance/Resilience
- Balance of time and intensity of an activity
- Time, place, and people for doing activities and humor
- Balance/moderation
- Understanding value

3.) LEARNING ABOUT CONTRIBUTION IN ORDER TO RELATE TO OTHERS

- Consideration
- Contribution
- Value for others belongings

Stay focused on accomplishing these in rank order first, meaning if your child is physically aggressive and struggles with personal space, ONLY FOCUS ON THIS PRINCIPLE. DO NOT TRY AND ACCOMPLISH TOO MUCH TOO FAST. Safety for a child and others requires a lot of attention and focus.

If you try to mix contribution principles and personal responsibility principles, you will overload the child, and they will escalate in physical violence even more. Less shitty parents tend to focus on ONE PRINCIPLE AT A TIME. Write down the 3-4 principle concepts that you and your co-parent believe are important to instill in your children in order of most important to least important.

So, the next question is, what do I do next? Telling them the principle isn't going to make them pick up the backpack by itself. Hell no, of course not! What is this, amateur hour? Head on over to the next chapter so we can talk about some ingredients you will be learning more about to be the less shitty parent you came here to be.

Dos and Don'ts

So, let's go over the dos and don'ts of this chapter so you can take clear action steps.

Do

- Start to recognize how much compliance you find yourself falling into and identify how this is unproductive.
- Start to highlight with your partner ways in which they are also falling into this trap. Work together as best as possible as this is a tough transition.
- Identify the principles that you and your co-parent are going to start with and identify the others that you want to focus on after this one gets traction. Remember, no more than 4!
- Start working on being more emotionally validating. If you are having a hard time understanding this, please checkout my YouTube channel with more information. I also go over more in later chapters on validation.

- Remember to be patient and recognize that this perspective shift will take some time for both you and your co-parent to get. Be compassionate.
- Let your child start to have more opportunities for autonomy and independence in order to give them the ability to learn without you being reactive or trying to save them/help.

Don't

- Keep focusing on compliance and the problem language.
- Continue to engage in long winded lectures. Try to stay focused exclusively on the principle.
- Get defensive or guarded when being challenged by your co-parent. They are your ally in this and if they are trying to help you recognize that you are falling into old patterns this is incredibly helpful.
- Focus on having too many principles at once. You can also accomplish the important ones and add on in the future.
- Think that this chapter alone is going to stop these behaviors. It is only meant to assist in cutting back on the amount of ridiculous content arguing.

Chapter 6

HIGHLY EFFECTIVE STRATEGIES TO BE LESS SHITTY

In this chapter I am going to go over some of the raw ingredients that you will be required to utilize if you want to become a less shitty parent. These are counterintuitive and take practice. Be patient with yourself. You are already shitty so there is no need to put pressure further onto what you are already doing.

At the end of this chapter, you will be able to…

1. Further understand validation without accommodation.
2. Understand how normalizing negative experiences can improve kids' resilience.
3. Use "and" instead of "but" to cut down substantially on emotional reactivity in your kids.
4. Identify traps that all parents fall into that lead to dead end power struggles.

5. How to use a tone of indifference that does not contribute to the victim mentality in kids.
6. Use the power of open ended, emotionally reflective questions.
7. Positively prophesy to believe in your child being capable.

What is Validation?

First thing I teach parents is to verbally validate, but not physically or emotionally accommodate. In short, validate, but don't accommodate. We first need to understand validation and what it is and isn't.

Validation is understanding a person's emotional experience based on the aspects of the experience that they are focusing on. Just because you can understand someone's experience and validate it DOES NOT MEAN THAT YOU AGREE with their overall perspective. It just means that you can understand how they could experience or feel something based on what they are focusing on.

An example may be that your child comes home from school and feels that the teacher was bullying them in front of the whole class. Now when you ask them what happened, they tell you that the teacher told them to stop talking with their friends, who they were trying to help out as they were going through a breakup. Your child feels that the teacher was cold and rude, when they were trying to just help their friend. They also could feel as though the teacher was socially shaming them and embarrassing them even though their intention was to be supportive to their friend.

Validation would sound like this: "Hey, I can totally understand where you are coming from. Your friend was hurting, you wanted to be there for them and didn't want them to feel alone. You're trying to be a good friend. You felt that the teacher wasn't being as sensitive to the situation as you were. I get that ***and*** I think the teacher didn't have the context and it was probably distracting for them to try to teach while you guys are going through your friend's breakup. It could have been the wrong time and place to talk with your friend about their breakup."

Do you see that at NO POINT do you identify that the teacher was bullying them?

You also <u>DO NOT</u> accommodate the behavior *even though the child felt as though it was justifiable based on their friend's feelings of being hurt and needing support.*

Other examples of this can be more behaviorally concrete, such as this:

Your kid comes home from school and drops their backpack in the middle of the living room floor and runs off. You stop them and say, "Hey I know you had a long day at school and are excited to go play video games or chill out. I want you to be able to do that too ***and*** can understand why you may have just left your bag here, not realizing it in the rush to go relax. This is a great opportunity to have consideration for others that have to be in the living room and know you will make the right decision."

See how I am validating, but not accommodating the inappropriate behavior. I am making an educated guess and trying to give the benefit of the doubt as we previously discussed.

Now listen, I am not naive in thinking that this is going to just magically get your kids to follow through on embracing the principles you set forth. We will be discussing leverage and strategic consequences shortly. I just want you to be able to recognize how this could be a short and simple strategy to reduce giving too much negative attention and engagement to your kids.

Pro Level Tip!

If you notice above I have bolded, underlined, and italicized the word "and" because usually parents use the word "but". This one word has a significantly and utterly insane powerful shift on how it impacts your child. When you use the word "and" instead of "but", it connects two opposing ideas and makes them equally valued. When you use "but", it disconnects and diminishes the child's experience, thus giving them the impression that their feelings, perspectives and all the validation that you just did was complete bullshit. This is incredibly powerful if you can start to utilize this strategy to really stop or at least diminish the pushback you get from your kids.

Normalize the Negatives

Less shitty parents also are able at recognizing that the normal status quo of life is pretty baseline negative. People being hurtful, tired, having a hard time overcoming a challenge. All normal! Yet, today we can't even stand in a Starbucks line...we mobile order. I too am guilty of being a total sissy and whining about this. Lines are NORMAL, PEOPLE! C'mon! I used the example of the computer at the introduction to illustrate this point too. This means we as parents and adults are responsible for creating reactions that are appropriate to the stressors or experiences kids have.

The best way to accomplish this is to be able to have a normalized tone and relaxed body language. This makes up for 93% of all communication.

Make statements, such as...
"It's really tough that you went through that and it's completely normal."
"I hear how that made you feel and it's also that it is completely typical that this is going to continue to happen."
"It's understandable that you had that feeling and that's typically how people can be sometimes."

See how these strategies are not minimizing your kids, but also not allowing their feelings to dominate the reality? Phrases like this, a validation coupled with a normalization response, using the word "and", are most appropriate.

A STEP-BY-STEP PROCESS ON HOW TO BE A LESS SH!TTY PARENT

Shitty parents tend to not validate at all and skip right to going in the opposite direction of normalizing.

They may completely jump to the child's emotional experience and take it as gospel. Saying things such as…

"Oh my goodness I can't believe that they said that to you!"
"I am sorry that you had to go through that."
"We need to make sure that this never happens again. We need to get this to stop!"
"I know this is truly horrible, isn't it?"

I want to make sure that you are fully understanding what I am saying here. I am trying to make sure that you do not fully buy into what the emotional experience is of the kids and overreact to make it worse than it was. I still want you to be able to validate their feelings and perspectives, without overreacting to them. This all too often creates and unintentionally creates a victim mentality in the child and continues to perpetuate a self-defeating narrative that the world happens to them, instead of through them.

Other parents may go in another direction by focusing on completely minimizing the child and their experience, almost going in the opposite extreme. This may give the child the impression either their feelings don't matter or that they are not being believed in their experience. Regardless, you <u>DO NOT</u> want this.

Some examples are...

"There is no way that this happened. Even if it did happen, you just need to move on."

"Get over it. These things happen all the time."

"Stop complaining about this. I have been through worse and I am fine." (Heard this one in sessions too much with clients.).

"You will survive. Let's look at the bright side..."

"You're being ridiculous and overly sensitive."

"Stop it."

Both of these approaches either invalidate the child extensively or they play into the experience as a helpless victim. Their limited life experiences and developmentally appropriate response of emotional processing can become distorted and confusing. Less shitty parents assist kids in helping them understand their emotions, develop appropriate personally responsible reactions, and work on them creating stronger character. This cannot be accomplished if we are overly reacting to their feelings and experiences as them being consistently victimized or by minimizing their experience in order for them to move beyond the experience.

This now leads me to the next strategy that will allow you to be able to create a healthy distance between you and your child emotionally.

A STEP-BY-STEP PROCESS ON HOW TO BE A LESS SH!TTY PARENT

Parents Struggle with a Tone of Indifference

Now, this strategy is going to definitely help you allow your kids to no longer have delusion leverage over you. Shitty parents have significant verbal reactions and emotional reactivity towards their kids when they talk back, lie, or start to make poor decisions. These tones tend to give kids the impression that you are emotionally bothered and upset with what they are doing, thus giving them the impression they can control and influence your emotional state and behavior. This is a dangerous game...

As many of you may have already experienced, the child will tend to do whatever you DON'T want them to do anyways, and they gain the added benefit of thinking that they are getting one over on you. This gives them a perception of power and influence. Something that I went over at the beginning of the book all kids want, remember?

Not only that, but we as the adults and authority are also modeling terrible emotional responses that are, I can guarantee, giving your kids the impression that they are acceptable for them to have. This in turn becomes hypocritical and creates even more of a desire from the child to lash out and create escalating power struggles again in the future.

Lastly, this also can create scenarios in the long term where a child will do self-destruction and physically harmful behavior in order to retaliate and get back at their parents. This is something that I have seen all too often in my cases. The kid will purposely sink their grades knowing that it will frustrate the overly involved and emotionally enmeshed parent who all they care to talk about are the kids' grades. This then ruins their chances of having future options potentially for education and beyond.

When parents start to have a tone of indifference and make statements that are validating, but not accommodating, it allows the child to have to bear the brunt of their choices and no longer gain the emotional and delusional gratification that they are getting back at their parents for. Obviously, this needs to be practiced and implemented over and over again for the desired effect, but once consistently implemented with accountability, kids start to recognize that they are only doing it to themselves. There are limitations to going deeper on this topic in the book so if you want to learn more about this and what it means, please check out my Youtube channel, Matthew Maynard, LMFT for my free video that explains this.

But Matt, I have heard from other experts I shouldn't yell *ever*, is that what you are saying?

No, this does not mean that you never yell. I am a big believer in your kids getting reprimanded and yelled at. Kids today need to know that there are lines. Once those lines are crossed, they need to know that things that happen after are largely out of their control. This further reinforces a hierarchy.

Some examples of appropriate times to yell are...
- Major safety concerns. (Running into the street, trying to topple something heavy over, etc.)
- Once your child has crossed a major boundary numerous times they need to recognize the inappropriateness of this. (Going into your bedroom without permission, touching

belongings that are yours and they should not be using them, disregarding the consideration of others over and over again).

Yelling is a tool. It's a tool that can be utilized effectively if used sparingly. Like any tool overused it will degrade over time and become less and less effective. The goal is to use this at times where you really need something to sink in that you have tried to get it to sink in in other ways first. Less shitty parents recognize these opportunities and manage themselves better in situations that I described above.

I got something better than yelling, though, that can create a breakthrough in engaging your child to shift a behavior. It's called positively prophesying.

Area's Parents Engage in Dead End Power Struggles

Name Calling and Back Talk

There used to be a saying that says, "sticks and stones will break my bones, but words will never hurt me". Do you remember hearing that as a kid? It was a great mantra and to this day should still ring true…unfortunately, it does not. If the saying were calibrated for today's times, it would go something like this: "Sticks and stones will break my bones, and words are more violent and crushing my soul." Parents I work with also don't follow the old mantra and have bought into the new one I came up with. They say funny things like, "I am not going to let them talk to me that way" or the classic, which I LOVE, "If I ever spoke to my parents that way, they would have killed me!" Please, for the love of God if this is you and you are one of these parents, I desperately want to impart some wisdom on you. Words are meaningless. They are cheap. They are attention seeking at their most basic of levels. They cannot do anything to you except wound an already insecure part of your ego. IF that's the case, please address it! Your kids are going to say terrible, awful things to you that I can tell you they NEVER MEAN! I've heard some heinous things from kids, and I can only promise you that it is primarily for attention seeking and because they are hurting. They rarely mean the things they say.

So, I want you to make me one promise by the end of this book—that you will raise what I call your TOGAF. It's an acronym for "Threshold of Giving A Fuck". Words are so low of a threshold to care about that you need to definitely raise the level of things you respond to with your kids.

I always joke with the parents that I work with when we come to this part in my coaching that they must buy their fucks in bulk at Costco because they clearly have an abundance to waste! Please stop buying them wholesale and start buying them at a premium at a convenience store. Raise your TOGAF and I can promise you this one thing alone will help improve whatever the situation is specifically with your family.

Lastly, I want to highlight the importance of freedom of speech. This is an incredible freedom that some are taking for granted or trying to turn into the concept that words are oppressive and violent. This is nonsense and history can also tell you that the silence of speaking out or stopping debate on topics has only led to more oppressive and terrible outcomes. We also need to start to teach our children this concept as we are watering down their ability to move past others perceptions of themselves and instill a stronger sense of self and identity. Please model this for your kids as it is truly a sign of strength and resilience.

Instead, the principles that you may address might be managing disappointment, consideration, or accepting "no". Highlight this by saying something like,

"Hey, I understand that you're disappointed and frustrated. That's ok. Remember you are still working on (insert principle here). We know you are going to come up with some strategies to work through how you're feeling." You can also positively prophesy and validate their feelings more. This validation approach tends to work very well as this is usually what leads to most kids using inappropriate language or name calling. They also may be trying to engage in this language as they are attempting to draw you into a power struggle or get a reaction. You can also use the strategy of highlighting your old pattern and response in order to validate that it won't work. You can say something like this…

"In the past, this is usually where mom and I/dad and I would start demanding you to stop, start arguing with you about your language, take this too personally, or start threatening you.

Lying

Lying is an interesting concept and predicament for parents. Most take it overly personally and it results in them more often than not interpreting their child as thinking that they are stupid. Trust me, it's not personal, it's a gamble! There is a chance they can get around something that they don't want to do! The odds are always against them, but they try anyway! In all honesty, they think that what they are getting around is something for YOU! NOT FOR THEMSELVES. This is why some kids will start blaming parents when they don't do something they need to or do something that you told them to do in the past and say, "Why didn't you remind me?", "Why didn't you tell me?". If you are wondering where this came from, it's from compliance-based red herrings.

Anytime that you catch your child lying, remember they are only lying to whom? Themselves. Yes, they are technically lying to others, but the only one the lie truly harms is themselves as the reality or consequences of their lies always come back to haunt them! So, start this process early by saying something like this instead of taking it personally...

"Listen, we believe that you are lying about X, just remember though this is only for your own benefit so the only person that you are lying to is you. You know you are capable of doing x and we know it too." Obviously, we are going to use consequences to reinforce them sticking to a principle later instead of focusing on the lying. *Lying is a problem that is going to need to be turned into a principle.* That could be persevering, prioritizing, or managing disappointment, to name a few. You can go through the principles list and identify which ones work for you and your family dynamic. I am going to go over leverage and consequences shortly. I know you are anxious to get there but stick with this chapter first so it all makes sense.

And lastly, inappropriate, or foul language.

I am not condoning tolerating or letting your kids talk poorly. I have a sailors mouth at times (look at the title of this book), and I can also tell you that I understand the principle of time, place, and people. This may be the principle that you focus on instead of foul language or getting them to manage their language. Duct taping their mouth, yelling at them, and threatening them will only fuel the fire, as I am sure you are aware. These approaches also lead to you turning them into victims or controlling them, both of which we are actively trying to undo. Correct? Kids also like and want to feel more mature. They want to feel grown up. Even though we can all agree being an adult has some significant downsides, they think that it is glorious! Anyone want to trade with their kid?

Instead, focus on another red herring—highlighting the principle of time, place, and people. You can say something like this: "This is an opportunity/chance to recognize time, place, and people. I know you hear other kids maybe using this language and at times mom and I/dad and I may slip up. We also can understand you are trying to be more mature by using this language. We know you can start to recognize this more." Then disengage. Once again, we are going to use consequences and leverage at a later time to highlight this if your child continues to miss the chance to see the principle of time, place, and people. DO NOT HOLD THEM ACCOUNTABLE FOR SWEARING OR INAPPROPRIATE LANGUAGE. Principles over problems, remember? Plus, freedom of speech is one of the greatest freedoms Americans enjoy. We want our kids to understand and value this principle in its entirety. Unfortunately, the value of this freedom is being degraded in America with individuals claiming words are violent and oppressive. This isn't helping our kids develop grit and resilience if we are teaching them that.

The Power of Open Ended, Emotionally Reflective Questions

Less shitty parents ask open ended questions and prompt reflection and responsibility taking. Shitty parents ask leading questions like they are a cop interrogating a murder suspect! I want you to start practicing immediately ways you can turn "yes" and "no" questions into open ended questions. I also want you to go back and remember a few pages ago where I spoke on tone of indifference. This in combination with open ended questions, is incredibly powerful because it no longer gives your child the impression you are trying to get them to confess and admit fault in order to make them feel guilty or ashamed. We want your kids recognizing their own feelings, impulses, and rationalizations.

What were they thinking?!?!? News Flash…they weren't thinking at all!

If you are still trying to understand the logic behind your child or teen's behavior, please stop now. This is actually the last thing that they wind up getting to, and you can call it thinking with a loose definition if you would like. It is more like rationalizing and justifying.

When a kid acts inappropriately, the first question parents ask is, "What were you thinking?" Remember when they said in school there is no such thing as a stupid question…well this might be pretty close. Your kids were reacting and responding to their emotions and completely skipped over the part of their brain that focuses on problem solving.

The more appropriate question we are going to ask is, "What were you feeling that led to you making that choice?" This is the first question you will always ask. It is the beginning of where all problematic behavior originates. When your child responds, you are going to implement a substantial amount of *emotional validation*. This is a skill you will be learning much more in depth after I talk about these questions.

Example: "I can understand how you felt frustrated and annoyed that your dad asked you some questions about your day after school. You had a long day and you just needed some time to decompress before getting into your busy afternoon schedule."

The second question you are going to ask is, "Even though you felt that way, why was your behavior inappropriate?" This will allow your child to connect that the emotional trigger is understandable, but the response is inappropriate. Once they answer, you are going to highlight the principle concept that the inappropriate behavior was tied to.

Example: "Even though you felt frustrated with dad, why was it inappropriate to tell him to shut up and leave you alone?"

Give them a chance to answer. If they choose not to answer or say the infamous 3-word sentence that is gospel, "I don't know", highlight the principle.

Example: "Listen, we have been talking about you learning more about being considerate and this was an opportunity to apply that."

Lastly, you are going to ask them "What can you do differently next time you feel this way, so that you are not going to need to be held accountable?" and then say nothing. That's right. Don't try to come up with ideas with them. Do not try and give them directions to follow. Do not, do not, do anything. If they continue to say, "I don't know," which they invariably will at some point in this process, you are going to say, "This is clearly something to think about as this is a problem you are capable of solving." This is critical, because it highlights an appropriate boundary and an area of growth the child needs to build upon.

Example: "In the future, when you're feeling frustrated with dad, what can you say in order to still show consideration for dad?"

Positive Prophesying

Less shitty parents believe that their kids are capable of overcoming challenges and are going to do better in the future. At heart, they truly believe that they are capable and competent. Shitty parents nitpick and are hyper focused on details and setbacks, even though setbacks are normal. They unintentionally do not realize that they are inadvertently giving their kids the message that they DO NOT believe in their capabilities and don't think that they are competent on their own. This then leads to them becoming either spiteful and vindictive, or they become helpless and dependent. I am sure you don't want either. Am I right?

So, what is positive prophesying? It is the ability to believe that your child will eventually get a strategy or the perseverance to overcome a challenge. It's faith. Kids look to parents all the time to identify what is realistic and possible and what isn't. They use parents as a calibration tool for reality.

A great example of this is if a kid falls on the playground, scrapes their knee, and comes running over crying with some blood on their pants. The child's emotional response will either increase exponentially or decrease faster based on how the parent responds. If the parent responds anxious and worried with their expression, the child may interpret this as the leg needing to be amputated off. If the parent is calm and talks in a matter-of-fact tone of voice, the child may calm down faster as the parent is treating it as a small problem and therefore giving the child the impression that it is such, regardless of the physical pain.

I am going to help you use this to your advantage after you have gotten your child to answer the emotionally reflective questions we just went over. You need to believe that they will _eventually_ be able to implement their strategy. Obviously, this process is going to be a rough one as most kids need to fail multiple times and try to escape because they have been so dependent on their parents and accommodations for so long. This is something that will help fill in that feeling of needing to "parent" in these moments when the child is melting down, crying, or begging you to "give" them another chance. Remember, we are separating ourselves from the child's outcomes and emotions in order to start to create self-esteem that is more than likely desperately needed.

In application, it will look something like this:

"That strategy you came up with should be extremely helpful for you in the future. I know you are capable of doing it."

But Matt, what if their strategy is something that is unrealistic or involves me? Well, in these cases you are going to say something such as this…

"I know in the past we would have helped you and unfortunately this wasn't actually helping you. We are not going to be able to be a part of your strategy. You can come up with something that you can do on your own."

Keep in mind that their strategy can also be something that they think is a vindictive or spiteful act to you. I have seen numerous kids make up strategies in order to get back at their parents for "not understanding" or "not listening" to them. If your child is trying to do this, just say to them something along the lines of this…

"It's ok to be upset and frustrated. We know you are capable of coming up with a strategy that is realistic and is going to help you. Trying to get back at us or get us upset isn't going to get us to go back to the old pattern."

You can also highlight that they are only making things harder for themselves and that ultimately their own decisions and choices are for them and no one else. This process is meant to soften the blow of no longer accommodating and enabling the child.

Dos and Don'ts

So, let's go over the dos and don'ts of this chapter so you can take clear action steps.

Do

- Start to validate a ton. Supplement this verbal affirmation and understanding instead of enabling or engaging in fixing the problem.
- Recognize the ways in which you fall into power struggles with your kids lying, using foul language, or backtalking/name calling.
- Start and work on your tone of indifference. This is one of the hardest, but most effective strategies within this entire framework.
- Start to normalize the negative experiences that will naturally occur for your kids.
- Use the word "and" instead of "but". Work alongside your co-parent to master this.
- Positively prophesy as much as humanly possible.
- Validate past behavior that you engaged in that your child may be anticipating and trying to trigger in you in order to reduce the conflict from escalating.
- Start to recognize how emotionally reflective questions could be more beneficial than lecturing.
- Checkout my YouTube channel for more information. Just search Matthew Maynard, LMFT

Don't

- Get caught up in the three areas that parents fall into power struggles. (Backtalk, lying, and foul language)
- Yell unless there is a serious need (i.e. physical safety).
- Invalidate their feelings and experiences.
- Get reactive if your co-parent is trying to assist you in these new approaches and aspects to be more aware of.
- Be judgmental or critical towards one another as you are attempting to implement more of these strategies. Try and use some on each other as well, such as validating.
- Stop reading now! We are just about to get to the really good stuff!

Chapter 7

UNHEALTHY BOUNDARIES TO STOP DOING

Boundaries are one of the most important aspects of kids feeling confident and comfortable in a family system. By definition, a boundary is, "a line that marks the limits of an area; a dividing line." We must understand healthy physical and emotional boundaries. Most parents that I work with have substantially unhealthy and pretty significantly broken boundaries with their child. A healthy physical boundary is one in which we are focused on having our own physical space and touch. It gives us space to interact with others in a way that gives autonomy at times and closeness at others.

At the end of this chapter you will be able to…

1. Understand the difference between shitty boundaries and healthy boundaries.

2. The emotional impacts on healthy boundaries that seem counterintuitive based on the childs reactivity.
3. Why telling your kids you're proud of them sends a confusing boundary and what to do instead.
4. The trap of negative and unnecessary attention and engagement parents give.
5. Why parents continuing to care more about fixing problems for their kids is creating a victim mentality.
6. Recognizing the power of doing "nothing" and allowing space for your child's decisions play out.

Some examples of shitty boundaries in a family will look something like:

- Children are allowed to use the master bath/shower because they enjoy the space more.
- Children sleeping in the parent's bed or bedroom.
- Parents sleeping in their children's bed or bedroom.
- Children are able to enter into their parent's bedroom whenever they want, regardless of whether they have permission or not.
- Children take money, credit cards, cell phones, and items from their parents because they want something.

When these spaces don't have boundaries the hierarchy of the family comes into question. The child can interpret mistakenly that they are on the same "level" as the parent, resulting in them being rude and disrespectful. They can also go in the opposite direction resulting in them needing the parent in order to feel safe or comfortable when stressed. Either of these sound familiar?

A healthy emotional boundary is what allows us to stay independent and self-sufficient for meeting our emotional needs. It separates our wants, needs, and feelings from others. It also allows us to <u>not</u> take on emotional responsibility for others when they are feeling upset, angry, or hurt.

Some examples of cases I have worked on have been:

- Parents take over the child's ability to problem solve how they are going to start an essay because they are overwhelmed. Some even go so far as to write it for them! (No, I wish I was being dramatic).
- The child blames the parents for a poor grade they received from a project that they worked on collaboratively.
- The parent becomes anxious and overwhelmed when the child struggles with a peer at school or on a sports team.
- The child becomes unable to sleep on their own problems without major emotional outbursts, essentially making the parent sleep with them in perpetuity.
- The parents remove the child from situations in which they are in emotional duress or could be in emotional duress because of their own past experiences. (Good old-fashioned projection!)

Positive emotional boundaries, however, lead to self-esteem, pride, and dignity. Any assistance or emotional pity towards individuals unintentionally reinforces beliefs that they are incapable or incompetent of handling emotions. Displaying pity and sadness for a child can send them some serious mixed signals. It can eventually lead to dependence and support that is unsustainable and unrealistic over an extended period of time. This can then manifest in depression, anxiety, negative perceptions of oneself, and major interpersonal problems within a family dynamic. Longer term problems can be substance abuse, codependent/unhealthy relationship dynamics, domestic violence, etc.

Boundaries need to be instilled fully, as they are necessary for the child to start to take more responsibility for their own choices, their emotions, and their outcomes for them to have a happy and balanced life. Healthy boundaries also allow you, as the parent, to start to be viewed as an authority again, instead of an equal.

Why You Shouldn't Say You are Proud of your Kids First...

Shitty parents believe that them telling their kids that they are proud of them is a great thing...and honestly, it's terrible. Your pride in your children should be secondary to them first being proud of themselves. This is a major emotional boundary that is commonly overlooked because the intention is so positive.

Think about it. If you and your other parent are always focusing on how proud you are when they make good choices and show good behavior, that's for YOUR self-esteem...NOT your kids'! It's not coincidental that the word self is in self-esteem because only you can gain it by your own actions! If you are always talking about how your pride lies in your child, think about the pressure and stress that this can put on them. If they don't have a great relationship with you, they may actively do things that go against their self-esteem to spite you! This is insanely true of all the teens I work with. They may actively want to destroy your pride to try and get some space for their own development. This isn't rebelling, this is getting some healthy distance. They need to be proud of their own choices and behaviors for who they are becoming and want to be, not who you want them to be. From now on, say, "You should feel proud of yourself."

This will allow them to feel the esteem that they have created for themselves. It will also allow them to know that you recognize this. You can always end with something along the lines of this, "Obviously, we are always proud of you too", or "We are proud of you too."

This way, the pride that they are giving and getting from themselves is the most important and should be recognized as such. This allows your kids to also not become people pleasers or be abused by others who are constantly dangling validation, praise, and positive words of encouragement. The technical term is people pleaser.

Negative and Unnecessary Attention and Engagement

Kids are both master negotiators and telenovela actors/actresses. They love a good argument and will always over-dramatize the problems because they have limited life experience to draw upon to decipher what is a 2 problem on a scale from 1-10 vs an 8 problem.

Ay dios mio!

I am going to go over the ways in which we are going to use attention and physical engagement to our advantage to draw better boundaries. Shitty parents believe that their kids need more attention and engagement, and the brutal reality is that if you are reading this book and made it this far, your kids are getting more than enough. There is a lot going around on the internet that's leading parents to believe that this approach of giving more attention will solve the problem, but the truth is it is more than likely breeding a terrorist. Those who can relate please raise your hand!

Attention and engagement is like money to adults. You always could use more and feel that you aren't getting enough. In the introduction, I talked about how kids are seen, heard, prioritized, and given the impression that the things they do are always worthy of appreciation. This level of engagement is unsustainable, ineffective, and leading to a lot of unintended consequences like the rise of socialism as a great economic philosophy, politically correct cancel culture, and the rise of the use of "Karen" to refer to someone making some big deal out of something insignificant.

A STEP-BY-STEP PROCESS ON HOW TO BE A LESS SH!TTY PARENT

It's gone overboard and it's time we stop the shaming and guilting of parents and other adults to endlessly attend to the emotional and physical impulses of kids. Just because someone feels a certain way, DOES NOT mean it is a certain way. We have gotten confused over the course of the past 20 years about trying to validate children's feelings and perspectives as meaning we need to give into them or agree with them being the Truth with a capital T. This has led to a well-intentioned, but terrible approach of accommodating kids to an insane degree. There is an expiration on kids getting support in school and when it does end, we need to know they are prepared to be self-sufficient. I know that we have these accommodations in schools for kids with learning differences and I am all for them, so long as they value them, are able to persevere through challenges, and are taking more initiative over time to become more self-sufficient. Kids need to care more about solving their problems more than adults do. This is a main struggle that all the parents I work with say. "We care more about (INSERT PROBLEM HERE) getting fixed than they do."

Shitty parents keep believing that if they keep showing care and concern for their kids getting through a challenge or struggle, then eventually their child will. I have seen nothing but the contrary. The more the parent fixes their childs problems, the more the child is led to believe that others will care about fixing them as well. This delusion perpetuates itself in a variety of settings as time goes on. Shitty parents will indefinitely go out of their way to protect, insulate, and buffer the emotions of kids, resulting in lost opportunities to build grit, resilience, and perseverance. Less shitty parents are all about validating the kids' feelings and perspectives without accommodating them as much as they typically do or did in the past. <u>They realize that the child has to start to care more and more about their own choices, behaviors, and outcomes REGARDLESS of their challenges or feelings.</u> These less shitty parents focus on using this emotional strategy to help create breakthroughs in personal reflection and responsibility taking.

Doing Nothing and Saying Nothing is Still Doing Something

This strategy is the most underrated of all of them, but powerful for creating a strong boundary. There is a saying that silence is deafening. It's true, especially for kids. When you literally say nothing and do nothing, it sends a very strong message that the value of what they are saying or doing is not high enough to be engaged in. This teaches kids what is the appropriate or inappropriate way to gain attention and engagement from others. Unfortunately, as I spoke about in the introduction, we don't back parents up who are trying to draw firmer lines with their kids. Instead, shame and dirty looks are thrown towards them. I challenge you to remember TOGAF here and identify how many ridiculous or silly things that your kids say or do that you respond with in a serious and emotionally reactive way. Doing nothing is doing a lot. Active ignoring, walking away, putting in earbuds, or turning your back to them are all incredibly powerful. I have heard that this is modeling how to teach kids to be rude, but this is the furthest thing from the truth. You are modeling a boundary for yourself and that others will also do to your children in society. This is preparation for that reality.

Areas that I highly recommend doing nothing...
- dramatic flair when someone won't jump immediately to what they need (snack, water, ride to a friend's)
- getting reactive or angry because you will not help them find something.
- blaming you for something that is their responsibility and capable of doing themselves (sports equipment, water bottle, socks for a family vacation etc.)
- dialogue and answering questions when you have told them "no" regarding a request for something.
- emotional reactivity that is normally distressing and disappointing because these things happen in life.

Also keep in mind that the previous chapter I talked about those three areas you should stop falling into power struggles and let go of. Those are again disrespectful backtalk, lying, and foul language. I also expand on this in a YouTube video; just search "3 Attention Seeking Traps All Parents Fall For," or visit my YouTube Channel, Matthew Maynard, LMFT

Goals Without Deadlines are Delusions

Deadlines are a boundary. They establish when a child has made a choice to either engage and do what they need to do for themselves or that they have chosen to do nothing. That is their choice, and it is something I am going to help you start to respect. In the next chapter I am going to break down how this is important to establish in order to identify when you are either going to start enabling them or waiting until you have leverage to implement a consequence. Without establishing deadlines, you are creating an unclear boundary; without clear boundaries you have no parental hierarchy.

Setting deadlines is relatively straightforward. You want to give your kids opportunities to have flexibility around getting themselves ready and accomplishing tasks that they need to take more responsibility for. Use your best judgement with giving time for them to accomplish or complete something. Once that come to pass, you will either enable them and you will do OR you may do nothing and just let it ride a little bit longer to see if they accomplish the task.

How to identify if you need to enable or let things ride...

You will enable your child and complete the task past the deadline if it is going to create more chaos or problems for your life. An example with younger kids may be that in the morning your child is having a hard time getting dressed and coming downstairs to eat. You may set a deadline that they need to be downstairs in the next 5 minutes dressed and ready to eat. After that time has come to pass you will go up, grab an outfit and move forward with getting the child dressed. Once the deadline has passed they lose control of how the morning progresses because you more than likely need to be out of the house and on your way to work. Another example is if your kid makes a mess, and drops water, or leaves food lying around, you can't just let it sit there. It could bring in bugs, it could damage the hardwood floors, etc. You will set a deadline and after that move forward with picking it up for them. Don't worry though, in the future chapters I highlight how we are going to use accountability and strategic leverage to highlight a principle that they are struggling with in these two scenarios (consideration and cleanliness). In other situations, you may be able to let things play out and ride a bit more. The kid misses a deadline to get their laundry started and now they don't have the clothes they want for the next day. Natural consequence! Another one could be that the child misses a deadline to give a response to you about what they want from a take-out restaurant. You are not going to hunt them down and continue to ask them to look at the menu while they are playing video games. You may make an educated guess and move forward with ordering dinner. Once again, the principles here are perseverance and consideration.

Dos and Don'ts

So, let's go over the dos and don'ts of this chapter so you can take clear action steps.

Do

- An audit of the areas I outlined where you may need to establish more of a physical boundary for your kids.
- An audit of the areas I outlined where you may need to establish more of an emotional boundary for your kids.

- Highlight that they should feel prouder of themselves, and obviously you are proud of them too.
- Recognize the power of establishing boundaries in positive ways for your kids and your marriage.
- Establish deadlines in order for your kids to start to respect the family hierarchy.
- Start to limit the amount of unnecessary dialogue and engagement. Work on doing nothing!
- Tolerate some instances where your kids need to sit in some level of discomfort based on their own decision making or lack thereof.

Don't

- Fall into the pattern of giving more attention to overdramatic reactivity from your kids.
- Allow your kids to keep breaking boundaries that are not going to help you establish a new hierarchy.
- Stay locked into dialogue that is going to lead to further debates and arguments.
- Lecture and give longwinded responses and explanations.
- Beat yourself up! You got this. I know you do!

Chapter 8

TAKING RESPONSIBILITY AND SETTING A NEW NORMAL FOR HIERARCHY

Now is where we have the rubber hit the road and you finally admit to your kids that you have been pretty shitty.

We do this for a couple of different reasons.

1. You can drop some guilt and shame. Remember, though, you're going for less shitty so this will never leave.
2. You model taking responsibility. This helps your kids see it.
3. You and your kids can have a cathartic moment where you process what has happened in the past and have closure/forgiveness.

4. You strategically get ahead of your kids trying to leverage the past shitty behavior you have had against you in the future when we welcome them to consequences.
5. This is the first step to reaffirming the hierarchy so we can create stability.

My recommendation is to start off with a family dialogue to clear the air. Do it around something that is enjoyable and going to keep the kids interested in sticking around. Pizza, ice cream sundaes, before a movie night, etc.

Make sure that your dialogue has these elements to it.

1. You're taking complete responsibility for the problems in the family dynamic up until now and apologizing for any of your poor past behavior (i.e. hitting, screaming, swearing, threatening, breaking of items, etc.).

You're doing this again to model full responsibility and take away any unnecessary shame, blame, and guilt that you may have placed on the children. Also, this won't be able to be weaponized in the future to try and get you to feel bad or trigger you to react poorly in the old ways you may have. Lastly, it's just good modeling.

2. Highlight the principles and that these are going to be focused on from now on in order to create more harmony and happiness not only in the home, but also within themselves to help them feel more confident.

Remember we are giving them the principles and going over some examples of problems that you may have focused on. This allows you to also talk about how this can cut down on arguing details and semantics. Plus, it is simplifying what you may (and by may, I mean did) overcomplicate or poorly communicate in the past. Take some ownership here too.

3. Highlight that you are going to hold off on implementing consequences for a few days to adjust to them starting to reflect and recognize the principles.

You should do this as a good rule of thumb not only for your kids to acclimate but also you. It allows you to practice the emotionally reflective questions and to allow yourself the space to recognize how much you have been enabling and need to let things ride a little bit more. Remind them, however, that if there is blatant disregard for the safety of others, you will be implementing consequences (I.e., hitting, kicking, pushing, throwing objects, breaking items).

4. Ask them if they have any questions and remind them that this is about getting them to be empowered.

Answer these questions to the best of your ability based on what we have gone over in the book.

Now, during this time, I want you to just focus on validating their feelings and reducing the amount of enabling that you have done in the past. You may have to reread the last chapter in order to better understand the distinct differences between when to enable vs when not to. So please make sure that you remember this before you start rolling anything out.

You want to keep in mind that this process is solely focused on letting problems ride and play out. Implementing a new process takes a lot of time and you're fighting the homeostasis of the family dynamic. This is strong and I can promise that you may need some help from outside professionals like licensed marriage and family therapists. Tell them about this book and give it to them as a resource as they may not have heard about this just yet.

During the course of this week, I would recommend that you try and get your kids to answer those emotionally reflective questions. This is more than likely a fruitless venture, as most kids are annoyed or frustrated by these questions as they are so used to a couple of different things happening.

1. You just enabling them and doing it for them.
2. You screaming and yelling like a lunatic so they can blame you.
3. You forgetting about the problems and moving on because it's just more peaceful.

During this week, the only things that you should be saying and the closest to lecturing you should get is highlighting opportunities for them to embrace a principle.

Making statements such as…

"Hey, this is an opportunity/chance to embrace (insert principle here)."

"Hey, you may want to consider possibly thinking about (insert principle here)."

Then let it ride; see what your kids do. If you need to enable them because of what we went over in the previous chapter, by all means, do it.

Here are the emotionally reflective questions again.

1. "What were you feeling that led to you doing (x)."

   Then validate their feelings.

   "I can understand that you were tired and just wanted to relax after coming home from school." "I get it. You are annoyed by your sister because she has touched your stuff again."

2. "And even though you felt that way, why was (x) inappropriate?"

   Highlight the principle

   "It comes back to you being able to (insert principle here)."

3. "You're going to feel this way again in the future and we are going to continue to hold you accountable to embracing (insert principle here) so you are going to have to come up with a strategy for what you can do differently to not have a consequence."

Couple of things to remember when asking the emotionally reflective questions:

1. Don't expect them to answer these when they are in the middle of an emotional meltdown. Neurologically they are so hyper emotionally engaged that their ability to process thought is a delusion of grandeur. Wait until there is some space and time away from the event.
2. Don't expect them to want to answer these questions at all! Remember they are used to you doing almost all of the leg work. They actually are not being required to think and reflect. This is more work than most of them will do outside of school! Still try as it is good practice and it won't allow them to have an excuse when we start implementing strategic leverage to say we "did not give them a chance."
3. DO NOT USE THE WORDS WE, US, or OUR. This a major mistake a lot of parents make as they are still trying to show connection with their kids. Remember to exclusively use YOU. It is them who are going to have to shift on their own process. This is only about them and themselves.

During this week, continue to highlight opportunities to embrace the principles. They may get annoyed and frustrated with you always using the principles. That's the point and that is exactly how you know that this is working. They are hearing that these themes keep popping up. In a wide variety of situations, too!

Word of Caution...

During this process, they are going to try and antagonize and do what I call "poking the bear". Like a bear from hibernation, they want you to freak out and maul them so they can play the victim and not have to shift or take responsibility. Remember they can be less shitty than you; that gives them justification for whatever nonsense they are trying to pull. Beware of them trying to argue details, semantics, and content. They love this. They are like highly skilled lawyers trying to create something out of nothing.

Pro Tip: Whenever they try to do this, say, "All of that is true and remember it just comes back to us talking about (insert principle here)." They will continue to throw content and details out there like they are chumming the waters trying to get JAWS to breach the surface of the water to eat you. DON'T FALL FOR IT! Instead, just keep repeating what I stated above and then disengage. They are going to make their choice and you are going to continue to make yours, ultimately, in the future, establishing a strategic consequence.

All in all, this week should be somewhat toned down. The kids are still more than likely going to not answer these questions but remember to still try. If you have younger kids between the ages of 5-8, you may be pleasantly surprised as they tend to be empowered by the questions, and since you are giving them space to have more control, they love it! The older kids tend to be lazier and more entitled based on your old way of doing things, so don't be surprised at all if they have limited engagement. When they choose not to answer or give you the impression they are doing you a favor by answering, I want you to say this…

Pro Tip #2: "Hey, this isn't for dad and I/mom and I, this is a chance for you to reflect and take some pride in your choices so that you don't have to face consequences in the future. We respect your ability to make this choice because you want to learn to figure out what you want to do on your terms."

Saying this is extremely respectful and shows a boundary. This will only further reduce any sort of enmeshment or unhealthy boundary that is more than likely still present in your dynamic. This is also a good way for you to recognize the boundary as well. Use this as a chance for you to recognize what is still triggering you and start to take more responsibility for your own reactivity during this week. It really helps model that. Talking about it with your kids shows that you are also doing some reflection, so you don't look hypocritical. Remember to please read the next chapter before you roll this out as it goes over how this all comes together with consequences and understanding when to enable and when not to.

Dos and Don'ts

So, let's go over the dos and don'ts of this chapter so you can take clear action steps.

Do

- Create your family script to prep the "new normal" and don't forget to take responsibility for your shitty parenting approaches of the past.
- Find something that is enjoyable and will keep the kids around to want to hear you out as much as possible.
- Focus on this new process of interacting to have more fun and enjoyment as a family.
- Beat the principles during this week like a dead horse! Catch you and your co-parent falling back into patterns of problem focused reactions and remind them principles over problems!
- Look at areas where you can be hypocritical and improve on these areas. Remember you are a model.

Don't

- Try and keep pestering the kids to answer the emotionally reflective questions.
- Expect miracles of any sort during this week.
- Engage in long winded lectures and tirades.
- Fall into old power struggles or traps.
- Overly explain yourself and the dynamics that led to *your* past behavior after you have taken responsibility.

Chapter 9

STRATEGIC LEVERAGE VS TRADITIONAL CONSEQUENCES/ PUNISHMENT

Strategic leverage is something that is not very well understood by parents that I work with based on them being raised in compliance and emotionally entangled dynamics. This is ripe for them to fall into power struggles and fall into breaking the hierarchy that you and your co-parent may be so committed to strengthening.

Leverage is power. Without leverage, you have an equality in a dynamic, which is why parents fall into poor reactions such as…

- Yelling at them OR Trying to talk rationally
- Threaten OR Incentivize

- Quid pro quo (this for that) OR negative future quid pro quo (parents take something away that they have leverage over in the future)
- Intimidate the child OR Accommodate the behavior
- Berate and personally attack OR excuse and minimize the degree of the negative behavior

You get the jist. Before we talk about leverage, though, there is a major problem within all the dynamics above which is why parents are exhausted.

The parent cares more about this principle or situation being addressed than the child, thus they are enabling the behavior.

Enabling vs Support

The difference between enabling vs supporting someone comes down to one very simple factor: who is taking more consistent action and emotional interest in solving the problem at hand. If the parent is doing more action and becoming more emotionally invested in the outcome than the child, they are enabling. Plain and simple. If the child is emotionally caring and taking more action than the parents are, they are being supportive of the child addressing a challenge.

I cannot stress enough how imperative it is to understand this significant difference. IF you are currently enabling, please study this chapter substantially. You may also want to check out all of my YouTube material talking more about this as well as my Emotionally Strategic Parenting Audio Program.

When To Enable vs Do Nothing

"But Matt, if I stop caring as much as they do they will (insert problem here) and I will pay the price. I can't just stop all of my enabling because it will massively affect (insert adult problem here)."

Don't worry! I got you! You are going to enable them in this system only when the costs for not doing so have a substantial impact on us in our adult lives (work, family responsibilities to other children, etc.).

We are going to start charging them emotionally for the excessive enabling in order to start to create care. Costs=care.

Up until this point in your dynamic, I can promise you that based on my definition above you have massively cared way more in areas that they are capable of and need to face more negative consequences around.

Example: Your child doesn't get up well in the morning and if you don't go in over and over and over again to get them up, you will be late for work/appointments/prior scheduled engagement/self-care, etc. You will start to set deadlines and highlight that after those deadlines that they may face some level of accountability to (insert principle here; perseverance, consideration, initiative, etc.).

A goal without a deadline is a delusion.

So remember, tell your kids that they have until (insert time here to get themselves up in the morning) and if they choose not to get up then they may face some level of accountability. This will allow you to know that the child needs a consequence or more consequences in order to start to have them embrace the principles.

Going back to our morning example a parent may say something to their child the night before such as:

"Hey, tomorrow I am only going to come in at the last possible second for you to get up. That means I will be coming in at (insert time here). I am doing this because I don't want to take away the opportunity for you to show that you can (insert principle here). If you choose not to get up on your own, that's on you. I know you are capable of doing this and believe that you will come up with a way to do this."

This approach is loving, but also establishing a firm deadline. You are positively prophesying. You are highlighting that you recognize in the past this would take away a chance for them to get themselves up on their own.

What happens if they argue with the deadline and come up with something ridiculous?

Kids are always looking to test the limits! Remind them that you are not arguing with them and know that they are capable of meeting the deadline. Validate don't accommodate here and walk away after you have made this declaration. They want an audience and they want a power struggle.

Leverage Litmus Tests

Now that we have established when it is appropriate to implement a consequence and use strategic leverage, let me show you how to identify whether you have leverage or not.

I came up with these three leverage litmus tests as I was finding patterns throughout all the cases I was working with. A litmus test, for those who don't know what it is, is essentially a quick "yes" or "no" to identify whether you can move onto the next phase in a sequence. In this case, whether or not you can use a consequence.

The number one pattern I found with shitty parents that didn't have leverage would be to engage in a physical or verbal altercation to get access to a consequence. Examples include, grabbing cell phones/tablets out of their kids hands, asking for them to hand over their cell phone/tablet, or chasing their kids around their house to get their belongings they were using as a consequence. I once worked with a desperate mother who thought she ripped the kids' xbox gaming console out of the family room and smashed it on the front steps (I know shitty right?) in a fit of rage. She later found out, though, it was the $400 cable DVR box to which she had to pay to get fixed.

The 3 Leverage Litmus Tests

Based on this, the first leverage litmus test is this: Are you going to get into a physical or verbal altercation to get access to the consequence? If the answer is "yes", WAIT! If "no", move onto the next leverage litmus test.

Another hallmark power struggle was that shitty parents were using consequences that resulted in other family members experiencing the consequences even though they didn't do anything wrong. Some examples of this include not going out to dinner as a family because of misbehavior, parents canceling their date night in order to implement a consequence, a sibling missing out on an activity because they don't want to "reward" poor behavior of another child.

The problem with this is that it results in giving the child who is NOT embracing the principles the impression that they can control and influence the entire family. Talk about control! They friggin love this! Not only that it shows that they can also create havoc if they also don't want to engage in those social activities resulting in them actively finding ways to be disruptive and misbehaved.

Based on this, the second leverage litmus test is this: Are you going to socialize this consequence to other members of the family? If the answer is "yes", WAIT. If the answer is "no", move onto the last litmus test.

Finally, the last shitty parenting power struggle was around parents' emotional bandwidth to accomplish tasks that were imperative to their own well-being. Some examples include long drives in the car or plane traveling, significant tasks that needed to be completed on a deadline for work, travel plans for one of the parents that required them to sleep, etc. This DOESN'T mean the parents were tired and didn't want to deal with the child's reactivity to facing accountability. It means that they have something substantially more important for work or life that requires as much bandwidth as possible to complete for either safety reasons (driving) or for the survival of the family (work).

Based on this, the third leverage litmus test is this: Do you have the emotional bandwidth to accomplish what you need to for you as an adult and for the family's overall functioning? If the answer is "yes", WAIT. If the answer is "no", then implement the consequence.

You are NEVER threatening, informing, proactively telling the child, or giving them forewarning about the consequences being implemented. This is a shitty parenting move that a lot of other parenting approaches tout.

A few reasons this is a awful idea are:

1. It is a verbal power struggle (remember litmus test 1?)
2. It gives the child to ability to identify whether or not that consequence matters to them.
3. Your credibility of following through is probably shitty at best, and even if you have a history of being consistent with following through, it looks like compliance ;)
4. You are showing your hand and now using the element of surprise to create healthy amounts of anxiety for your child to start to be more reflective in the future.

"Matt, this is pretty messed up, though. I am just surprising them with a consequence?" Yup!

Not all anxiety is created equally.

You and I have healthy amounts of anxiety around getting pulled over by the police for speeding (some of you do, at least). This anxiety of not knowing when, and to what extent, you can face accountability for being caught speeding results in you (I hope) managing your speed through self-control. Some of us, though, have had to get pulled over to experience that anxiety.

Not knowing if the cop is going to be kind or a jerk? Not knowing if you are getting a verbal warning, a written warning, a ticket, asked to get out of the car, etc.? These interactions and anxiety allow for judgment and consideration, more often than not. Last I checked, they aren't pulling people over and giving them money when they catch them doing and following the speed limit, right? This is why you will NEVER hear me talk about incentivizing or rewarding average and standard behavior. It <u>DOES NOT EXIST</u> beyond your home and it is setting your kids and you up for a delusion for when the reality does happen where your kids are held accountable.

We are using consequences to create dialogue, not crush their souls.

This is where you are going to wait until your child has realized that they can't find or gain access to something they want. DO NOT inform them that you have taken it away. Wait for them to realize it. This is purposeful for 2 reasons:

1. It allows the healthy anxiety to develop
2. You do not look like you are using it to engage in a power struggle and be punitive or angry as you may have in the past.

Highlight once they realize you have the leverage that you are going to start off by holding onto this for a day to give them time to reflect on their choices and how they can come up with a strategy to do something different for themselves in the future.

Pro Tip: DO NOT USE WE, US , OUR or indicate at any time this has anything to do with you. This is where parents fall back into patterns of enmeshment and give the false impression that the child is doing them a favor by actually reflecting and taking on a new approach in the future. This leads to destructive entitlement. Instead highlight that you are holding them accountable to do what you know they are capable of doing different in the future.

Pro Tip #2: Positively prophesy and highlight that you in the past would have (insert failed parenting approach here: negotiated, argued, haggled, screamed etc). "In the past, this is where I would have been threatening you and arguing with you to just clean up after yourself and I told you that I am no longer doing that. It is understandable that you may have thought that was going to happen. I am choosing to not go back to doing that as it wasn't helpful for you helping yourself."

Wait 24 hours and then highlight for your kids that they have an opportunity to earn the privilege back by reflecting and embracing a strategy in the future. When it is convenient and not disrupting your adult responsibilities, you can ask them those 3 emotionally reflective questions.

3 Emotionally Reflective Questions

1. "What were you feeling that led to you doing (insert behavior here)?"

   Then I want you to use validation. Ex: "I can understand how you felt tired and really were nervous about going to school since you were being picked on."

2. "Even though you felt that way, why was (insert negative behavior here) inappropriate?"

   Then I want you to highlight the principle. Ex: "It comes back to you being able to (insert principle here).

3. "You're going to have these feelings again in the future so what can you do differently so that you don't have to face a negative consequence?"

   Then I want you to do something incredibly powerful. Say literally nothing. Don't give them any strategies or ideas. DON'T DO IT! It's a trap!

Remember, we want them to come up with their own approach so they can have pride, self-esteem, and care about their choices in the future. *Not only that, we don't want to be blamed if our strategy doesn't work because they half assed it!*

Progression OVER Perfection!

Since we are not trying to crush your kids' souls into compliance, we are looking for them to care more about their choices and following through on their strategy in the future.

Think of when you were teaching your kids to ride a bike or anything new. Initially, they are terrible. They fall over, they get nervous, they keep trying and slowly start to get the hang of it. This is NOT something fun, though, so the motivation is going to be limited.

These are the three criteria in which we are going to look to make sure to identify when we need to use consequences and when we are going to let things ride and play out.

1. Are they self-aware of the opportunities to embrace the principles? Meaning are they aware of the problem areas that you previously discussed and highlighted? IF you have already asked them the questions to identify a strategy, move onto the next area of progress. IF NOT, ask them the questions so that they can identify a strategy.
   <u>Reminder: their attitude and demeanor to answer the questions or going to give you a clear indication if they think that answering the questions are either for your benefit or their own. If they give you the impression answering the questions is for YOUR benefit, tell them that you can understand that based on you getting into power struggles before, but now this is for their own benefit, and you will continue to hold them accountable regardless.</u>

2. Are they taking future initiative on their own strategies with no prompts or reminders over time? Meaning are they taking initiative without you highlighting an

opportunity for them to embrace a principle? IF they are taking initiative, but still falling short, highlight that you see them starting to care more and let it play out a little bit. Don't implement a consequence right away. Let them get a hang of their strategy or come up with another one. IF NOT, definitely hold them accountable and use a consequence to highlight the need for them to take initiative in the future.

3. Are they getting more consistent with using their strategy more and more? IF SO, highlight the pride and the positive feelings that they are experiencing because they are no longer dependent on you. IF NOT, definitely keep using consequences if they are falling back into old patterns more often than not.

Less shitty parents use these three criteria as rough outlines along with their judgment to keep in mind you would rather your kids care and start to try more and more than get compliance. This process also highlights and gives flexibility and reality to your kids also overcoming challenges in other aspects of their lives as anyone who has achieved success in life knows that it is not a straight line. Think of a trend line when you are looking at the stock of a company. You are looking for whether that trend line since starting this process is moving upwards, or downwards, more often than not. If it is moving downwards, (the kid cares less than you do through action, their attitude and demeanor is one in which they think they are doing you a favor, or they are simply not persevering with following through on their strategy/answering the questions), then you will use consequences more and more over time. If it is moving upwards, (the kid cares more than you do through action, their attitude and demeanor is one in which they think they are doing themselves a favor, or they are simply persevering with following through on their strategy/answering the questions), you will want to wait to use consequences and instead positively prophesy and highlight that they should be proud for trying to figure out a strategy.

Consequences are like medicine that we need to titrate up to achieve a result by leveraging the law of attrition.

Most shitty parents go nuclear and take a ton of stuff away. Kids talking disrespectfully? "That's it, you lost screens for another day! You want to keep going? I can take more away!" Or they may start chasing their kid around the house, threatening that if they don't hand over their phones you are going to cancel Christmas! Sound familiar? They also just take all the screens away, all the dolls away, all the Legos away. They threaten to take away playdates at the last minute because of compliance. You get the gist.

First, you sound insane and unhinged if you take this approach. Sorry, not sorry. I understand the frustration, but remember what people who are governed by tyrants all eventually do…rebel!

Second, you are falling BACK into compliance if you are going into a mode where you are trying to get them to take a new action NOW. Remember, we are using accountability from this point forward, NOT compliance, in order to get them to be more empowered to come up and embrace their own strategies.

Third, you are setting yourself up to have to deal with a terrorist in the future. When they have nothing to lose, they have everything to gain by annoying, terrorizing, or creating emotional breakdowns that disrupt the entire family.

Does this ring a bell with either you or your co-parent? If so, let me show you how we can leverage consequences one at a time, and embrace a law of power that is strategic.

How are we using consequences differently?

We want to use one consequence at a time, and use time and more consequences over time, to improve the child's ability to get worn out by their own choices. It's based on one of the most powerful laws of power: the law of attrition.

For example, you may start off with a tablet as a consequence. The principle is still not being improved on and the child is not answering those emotionally reflective questions to get a strategy going. They may even give you the attitude and demeanor that they are doing YOU a favor!

Pro tip #1: I have seen this with every single case of mine based on the child still believing the pattern is about compliance. If this happens, validate that of course they think that they are doing you a favor because in the past, your approach, attitude, and body language gave that impression. You need to remind them at this point that they are only answering these questions to help themselves and that they are capable of figuring out a plan. Then ask again if they would like to answer the questions, and if the attitude or demeanor persists, disengage.

Pro Tip #2: Ask the emotionally reflective questions only once the child has calmed down. Never attempt to get them to answer these questions in the middle of a meltdown or argument.

Once you have asked the questions, they should have a strategy for the principle around that specific problem area. You should positively prophesy and move on with the day and wait 24 hours to have them have access to their privilege so that they can show that they are making progress on embracing the principles.

Pro tip #3: Ask these questions everytime you hold them accountable and when they are earning back the privilege in order to make sure you are reinforcing learning instead of compliance.

If you see them starting to act more and take more initiative with their strategy, but are still falling short, give them a break. *Remember, we are looking for progression not perfection.* You should continue to positively prophesy and encourage them to keep working at embracing their strategy. Remind them that this is only about them starting to feel more proud of themselves and being able to feel accomplished on their own.

You will rinse, wash, repeat this process in order for them to develop a strategy that they feel empowered in. You are also identifying if they are persevering to implement their strategy without being dependent on you at all. Lastly, you will be measuring consistency.

Consequences come in all different forms

Obviously, you are using things that you kids know and love. Phones, Tablets, Computers, TV, Toys, Cars/Boats, Bikes, Books (that's right!), dolls, etc. These are the easy ones and the ones I would start with. You are using consequences that are mildly frustrating and will get the kids attention.

I also instruct parents to remember to use attention and engagement more sparingly as most kids are still seeking negative attention at this point. Attention and spending time with them after an argument is also a consequence.

You and your family are going to be the only ones that will ever love them the most in life. It is YOUR responsibility to prepare them that others will not do the same. I am not saying that you give your kids the cold shoulder and be passive aggressive. I am also not saying that you do this in a mean, guilting, or shaming way. My recommendation for using attention and engagement should be disclosed to the child by saying something along the lines of this: "Hey I need some time to process my feelings after our interaction. I am going to be not talking or engaging with you until I am ready. I love you and I know you are learning to (insert principle here)."

This will allow you to establish the boundary, disengage, model what others will ultimately do to them in the real world, and lastly improve your perceived value from your kids.

Remind them to feel proud of themselves when they have success

Remember how I said earlier you shouldn't tell them that you are proud of them? Well this is where you start stating that they SHOULD feel proud of themselves. This step is often overlooked as most parents believe that the kid should be behaving this way anyways so saying anything seems like they are aggrandizing them. NOPE!

This allows you to start to highlight where the internal gratification process should start. As soon as you can, when they make great choices and you see them trying to overcome something that used to be emotionally difficult, implement this. Pride is a process to remember, so highlighting this in the middle of the process is massive for kids.

Sometimes, though, I have seen this backfire. Some kids are frustrated about going to the parenting approach because they feel like they have less control than they previously did. So, if you are getting backlash or reactivity, hold off on doing this for a little bit. Depending on the past dynamics and your approach, kids may feel you are being condescending or passive aggressive, especially if you have a reputation of being. If that's the case, you SHOULD validate that and say that you understand that based on your past reputation they are having a hard time believing you and you respect them for that. Remember not to get butt hurt here like you may have in the past for your kid talking disrespectfully. This is only going to ruin your credibility. Also, keep in mind that they may want to engage in a conflict just to try and get you to fall back into the same pattern as before.

Chapter 10

WHERE DO LESS SHITTY PARENTS GO FROM HERE?

I am not going to pretend at all that this book is going to give you a complete breakdown of what to do with your parenting. I wanted to create an overview for people to start to challenge a lot of the shitty status quo contributing to the mental health crisis in kids and adolescents in this country. So, please do not think for a minute I expect this to solve all of your problems. It, however, is a significant start.

The world that our kids are coming into is going to be so substantially different and complex than ever before. With the advent of the internet, 24/7 connectedness of social media, dopamine dumps with devices and games, and the global economic shifts dramatically changing, we need to upgrade our parenting approach for grit, resilience, and character. Character that will be timeless and withstand the ever-evolving focus on pleasure and immediacy.

We need to create unconditional character in our kids as this is one of the main ways they will be able to not only survive in adulthood, but thrive and contribute massively to the world, their family, and their community. We need leaders; right now we have too many followers. We have too many people who are looking towards others to solve their problems, to make them feel comfortable within themselves, and to place blame on others instead of looking inward.

I hope that this book has started you on the pathway to thinking differently about your parenting far beyond just behavior. I hope that this will give you a new set of strategies that goes against all the present delusions that have gotten us to this place socially and emotionally over the past three decades. Please remember that you are going to be largely alone when you start implementing this. People around you are going to think that you are breaking cardinal rules of parenting. This will make them insecure and more than likely critical and judgmental. I promise you this will happen as all my clients have experienced this firsthand when rolling this system out, but once they get results, people want to learn more. I want you and others to learn more. Please share this book with someone you lean on and someone that is a part of your community. Doing this in numbers has significant power and I promise you they will appreciate and thank you when they start getting positive results. I am warning you, though it's lonely at first.

Major Takeaways to Remember!

Here is an overview of things to remember that I can tell you I remind my clients constantly.

1. Review your family of origin and if need be, get yourself a good marriage and family therapist to go through it with. This can save you a ton of time and energy. It may also save your marriage and your family from falling apart. We all need help and there is strength in getting perspective.
2. The only real reason you are in this predicament isn't because you have failed, but because you have overachieved and done almost everything for your kids. Don't you dare keep beating yourself up.
3. Remember to laugh and have fun with your kids. We have become overly serious as I think there is a collective anxiety about children today. We have lost sight of why we have them; it is to allow us to be kids again without being weird! Please for the love of all that is holy embrace this as this has more value than anything in this book.
4. Rapport and emotionally attuning exclusively to what makes your kid them on an individual level is massive. Remember to lean into things that they exclusively care about as this will only serve your influence and authority in the future.
5. Validate, don't accommodate. Focus on validating their feelings instead of enabling the behavior.

6. Principles over problems! Keep the focus on the big picture and remember to not get hung-up on the details. Shitty parents join the devil in the details.
7. Goals without deadlines are delusions. Super important and one of the main reasons dynamics fall apart with my coaching clients. This should be he first area you troubleshoot.
8. Stop the threats and instead highlight the child making a choice. Choices and decisions are entirely our own. Help your kids own that instead of complying with you.
9. Remember the 3 dead-end power traps all parents fall for. Disrespectful language, lying, and swearing. Focus on the principle instead (consideration, managing disappointment, accepting no, time/place/people)
10. 3 Leverage litmus tests should be constantly analyzed. Are you making sure that you are using accountability by following these three leverage litmus tests? If not, you better get back to reviewing these!
11. Progression over perfection. Focus on them caring more about making progress so that they can keep the pride. We are not trying to crush their souls and be on the lookout for your co-parent who may fall into this due to resentment.

    a. *Progression follows three criteria. 1.) Self-awareness to the principles 2.) Taking future initiative on their strategy 3.) Consistency with embracing the principle in more and more areas.*

12. Positively prophesy. Always believe in your kids and know that they are capable of more than you can imagine. Give them the benefit of the doubt and champion them on. They will feel the pride and character strength they are going to need in this world.
13. Use "and" instead of "but". This one strategy can revolutionize how you think about conflicts and the complexity of the world. It will also allow two competing emotions and perspectives to exist at the same time. This is at the core of validation and love.
14. Recognize and stop the amount of lecturing, negative attention, and unnecessary engagement you give your kids. This is the main fuel for most fires parents are attempting to put out. Stop and restrain yourself. Doing nothing is sometimes doing everything.
15. Reprioritize your marriage and relationship with your spouse. This is something that can have a dramatic impact on escalating conflicts at first, but in the long run shows your kids that the hierarchy is more important at times than they are. This is critical to not creating self-centered kids. Remember there is no shame in asking for help.
16. Take responsibility for your own hypocrisy and own your poor modelling. You will feel better, your kids will learn how to be humbled, and empathy can be instilled for those who make mistakes and want to improve themselves.
17. If you are not asking the questions to have your kids reflect after they have been held accountable, **_you are_**

not following this system. You are just using a fancier form of compliance. Don't forget that the reflection and dialogue is the most critical piece to this entire system.
18. Recognize the times to enable and the times to let things ride. This is only to benefit you the parent and not emotionally to bail the child out. Be cautious not to let yourself fall into a pattern of feeling bad for your kids by enabling them because this may send the wrong message that you don't believe in them being capable.
19. Progressively raise consequences in time duration and amount in order to apply appropriate pressure for the lack of engagement in reflecting and applying their own strategy.
20. When you have implemented a consequence make sure you take responsibility for old patterns the child may be anticipating. (i.e. quid pro quo, haggling, negotiating, incentivizing, debating, siding, etc.) They need validation and recognition that these boundaries won't be crossed again.
21. Remember that you're going to suck and mess up a ton! So is your partner! So pretty please take it easy on yourself and your partner as change is hard and takes a ton of effort. You got this you less shitty people!

Need more resources?

Everyone that I gave this book to before I published it asked me for more resources. They wanted more and I am sure you may too. Please visit my bio site that has a ton of resources and opportunities for more content, most of which is free. I also have this book more in depth outlined through my parenting program on audio. It comes with a ton of additional stuff far beyond this book, including cheat sheets and resources that I could never fit inside of a regular book. You can follow me all over! Here are all my links and tags:

<u>Main Website with Freebies and More</u>
www.bio.site/mattmaynard

Instagram
@mrmattmaynard

Facebook
MattMaynardLMFT

TikTok
@mftmattmaynard

YouTube
<u>https://www.youtube.com/@mattmaynard</u>

LinkedIn
<u>https://www.linkedin.com/in/matthew-maynard-lmft</u>

I truly wish you and your family the best of luck! I appreciate you allowing me the honor of helping you, as I know you are taking a major risk trusting me with the most important part of your life. Thank you and I know you are on your way to being a less shitty parent.

References

1. Rao, U., Ryan, N. D., Birmaher, B., et al. (2020). Prevalence of Major Depressive Disorder in Youth: A Systematic Review and Meta-analysis. JAMA Pediatrics, 174(3), 259–268.
2. American Psychological Association. (2019). Stress in America™: Generation Z. Retrieved from: https://www.apa.org/news/press/releases/stress/2018/stress-gen-z.pdf
3. Substance Abuse and Mental Health Services Administration. (2019). 2018 National Survey on Drug Use and Health: Detailed Tables. Retrieved from: https://www.samhsa.gov/data/sites/default/files/cbhsq-reports/NSDUHDetailedTabs2018R2/NSDUHDetailedTabs2018.htm
4. Bridge, J. A., Asti, L., Horowitz, L. M., et al. (2018). Suicide Trends Among Elementary School–Aged Children in the United States From 1993 to 2012. JAMA Pediatrics, 172(10), 1018–1025.
5. Centers for Disease Control and Prevention. (2019). Attention-Deficit/Hyperactivity Disorder (ADHD): Data & Statistics. Retrieved from: https://www.cdc.gov/ncbddd/adhd/data.html

6. Lin, L. Y., Sidani, J. E., Shensa, A., et al. (2019). Association Between Social Media Use and Depression Among U.S. Young Adults. Depression and Anxiety, 36(6), 520–529.

Made in United States
North Haven, CT
27 February 2024

49318789R00088